Black Girl BAKING

WHOLESOME RECIPES INSPIRED BY A SOULFUL UPBRINGING

Jerrelle Guy

FOUNDER OF
CHOCOLATE FOR BASIL

PAGE STREET
PUBLISHING CO.

PAGE STREET
PUBLISHING CO.

First published in 2018 by

Page Street Publishing Co.

27 Congress Street, Suite 105

Salem, MA 01970

www.pagestreetpublishing.com

Distributed by Macmillan, sales in Canada by The Canadian Manda Group.

22 21 20 19 18   1 2 3 4 5

ISBN-13: 978-1-62414-512-4

ISBN-10: 1-62414-512-4

Library of Congress Control Number: 2017943529

Cover and book design by Page Street Publishing Co.

Photography by Jerrelle Guy

Printed and bound in China

TO EVERY BLACK GIRL
WHO CREATES HER OWN POWER,
IN HER OWN WAY

CONTENTS

SIGHT: SHAPES, COLORS AND PATTERNS • 12

AROMA: SCENTS AND CINNAMON • 48

SOUND: SNAP, CRUNCH AND MUSIC • 83

TOUCH: TEXTURES AND MOUTHFEEL • 118

TASTE: SPICE, HEAT AND FLAVOR • 156

The biggest difference between the ten-year-old me and the me right now is that my younger self didn't have space for speaking up and being bold, or even being seen. And my daddy was always there reminding me to watch myself, know my place and grow thicker skin. He needed me tough and smart enough to withstand the grating world he knew, but instead, I'd just slink away into my spaces of comfort, pull out a pencil to draw or write a poem about a girl, or find a big bowl of warm lasagna to sink my face into.

I've learned to stop apologizing for this part of myself. It's that very introversion coupled with my upbringing that has inspired this book. The collection of recipes I'm sharing are a mishmash of my life: my black roots, the Chamorro food my mother peppered throughout my childhood, the Caribbean islands that were my neighbors and the places my love for food has taken me to, including Italy, Texas, New York and finally, where I live now, Boston. New places are always opening my eyes and helping me think outside the box, but I always bring pieces of home with me as I move, and it helps me create a temporary safe space wherever I land.

A BIT ABOUT ME

I was born in a small city called Lantana in Palm Beach County, Florida. It was an interesting place to be raised. My memories of growing up there are rich, and I can't erase them, specifically the ones where food was involved.

Racism wisped westward through the beautiful draping palm trees off the east coast, landing on the left side of the city's bridge, leaving behind strife and social divide. It was like its own hurricane. But there was so much life on our side of town, and the food was infused with Jamaican, Haitian and Cuban culture—black beans and rice, fried plantanos, sautéed cabbage and carrots—and then of course, for me, the interwoven cuisines of both my parents.

My father, a Southern-born and -raised black man, has always appreciated a heavy plate, his meat front and center, and smothered in white sauces or brown gravies. That or something his mother would reel in on a rod that morning, scale and fry on her kitchen stove that afternoon. And then there's my mother, an island girl from Guam, who came from hard times and won't ever part from the comfort of salty, canned meats splayed over big bowls of sticky rice. Her tastes took hold of my tongue too, and now there's no stew that feels complete without a generous dousing of soy sauce and white vinegar.

And while I'd love to recite "the grandmother story," about how I'd stand at her hip, staring up while she stirred a pot of greens or mixed a bowl of battered bread as she'd narrate the next step in a recipe, there was nothing that felt romantic about watching her cook. It was something that was done because it had to be done. Whether she'd stretch breakfast eggs with a pinch of baking powder to feed a slew of us children, or pickle her green beans to keep them from spoiling, there was always a sobering sense of labor spilling over from her days on the farm back in Mississippi with her sister. And when she did take me fishing by the lake or canal to cajole some catfish for dinner, I never could keep up with her, snapping her twine and frustrating the hell out of her until she'd snatch the pole back. Big Ma's kitchen was a place where things happened in solitude. I never asked, she never really offered and I'd just wait for someone to tell me I could enter. The times I did stumble by or into it, I'd be left with an inerasable smell of dead sea-meat or the image of the kitchen floor scattered with old newspapers and fish scales. There was nothing romantic about it at all. It was practical business.

Food romance came much later, after years of bulk buying, cans and corner stores, after more years of honey buns, Jamaican patties, hot sausages, peas and rice, corned beef hash and many other things filled with sugar and salt. I remember we kept so many canned vegetables that I was the school hero in elementary school when the local can drive would launch—I had that box full to the brim.

I actually never grew a taste for green leafy vegetables and certain fruits until I started cooking for myself, which wasn't long after I stumbled on the magical world of the Food Network. I'd spend hours as a little girl watching butter and sugar cream together on screen, and fresh herbs get plucked from backyard gardens to go over platters of strange ingredients I'd never even heard of before. I didn't get lost in mythical J. K. Rowling novels like my sister did; I'd get lost in people's lush dinner parties or their decorated dining room tables filled with double batches of homemade desserts. I'd pass up a life filled with witches and wizards to wake up to a marbled kitchen countertop prepped with softened butter, glass canisters of sugar and flour and the purr of a KitchenAid stand mixer—preferably mustard yellow. And so that's the life I've chased ever since.

The power and self-control I gained from cooking things from scratch expanded my world, and it made me happier than anything. I'd put all of myself into the things I'd bake for people. And that's when people started to listen to me. I never felt I belonged to any one group—I was just communicating across them all, because something I'd learned early on is that everyone can gather around food.

BAKING WITH THE SENSES

Rules and precision aren't naturally my thing. I'm a hypersensitive baker, preferring to get lost in the smells and textures of food and the sizzling sounds they make while boiling in a saucepan or roasting under an oven's coil. So in this way, I'm not the baker you might expect; I've never studied under some tough-as-nails pâtissier in France to survive and tell the tale, and I also have really hot hands, a curse when trying to work cold butter into flour before it turns to mush. But my grandmother was a resilient baker—resourceful, intuitive and smart, and the thing that just recently dawned on me is that she never used a kitchen scale. Yet every Sunday her biscuits were spot-on, so tender and ready to be split to lie beneath a hard scramble of peppered eggs. May she rest in peace. After realizing that, I started to appreciate how much of the baking process is learning the way the food and ingredients should behave—the proper thickness of a yellow cake batter when my spoon is lifted, the smell of fruit when it's ripe enough to bake, the correct tackiness of dough for the bread or pastry I'm kneading—and how to set these things right if they're not already. It's something that just comes with years of practice—and failure.

I'd never even thought about getting a scale until I wanted to start baking for other people: my fluky cookie business post-graduation, and a few months ago when I agreed to write this cookbook. I froze up, started second-guessing myself, wondering whether everything I made had a texture that would please the baking gods. But boy, I tell you, life before those times was heavenly, and I was happily munching away at whatever unmeasured, off-the-cuff pie I threw together, and friends and family close enough to steal a slice would rave.

While there definitely are tips I've lifted from books and YouTube videos that help me understand why a cake collapsed or made my mouth pucker (too much baking soda, perhaps?), part of me enjoys making a fool of myself on the first go-round while botching a batch of whatever recipe it is I've dared to change and ruin. It's a moment of masochism that has made room for big waves of happiness and pride to flood in when it does come out perfectly and I've invented something new.

For many desserts, a recipe can only do so much anyway. Flour, eggs, ovens—they can all be so persnickety, can't they? I remember my first time trying to whip egg whites into lush meringue. It was a disaster I'll elaborate more about when I share the recipe for my Summertime Pavlova Pops (page 31). I spent weeks trying to get "silky, stiff peaks"—whatever that meant. It wasn't until I failed close to ten times, and moved away from the balmy Texas air, that I understood what silky stiff peaks actually were, what they felt like on my fingers and roughly how long my handheld beater had to run until they got there.

However, don't freak out, I will offer you all the exact weight measurements I use, because I understand how important they are, but I also encourage you to stop along the way to savor the sounds, colors, textures and smells that I noticed while writing them all down. For me, that's all the fun.

WHY THERE ARE VEGAN THINGS

I had so much internal conflict writing the recipes for this book. "To use egg or not to use egg?" That was always the question. And while some may consider egg to be the backbone of baking, for me, the question never had an easy answer.

Since the age of 4 or 5, when my belly finally disengaged the back zipper on my white church dress, I was officially overweight by everyone else's standards. And when I finally settled into "obesity" at 14, going "vegan" and cutting out entire food groups from my diet seemed like a good, albeit extreme, solution for my weight problem. While I began turning down some of the foods I loved as a child—cringing at the slimy viscosity of over-easy egg yolks, the kind my mother used to fry for me and sandwich between slices of soft white bread along with a thick squiggle of ketchup–I started to gain an appreciation for how delicious and satisfying dairy-free and egg-free versions of my favorite comfort foods could be. I started to appreciate desserts that weren't full or margarine and sugar and to love the natural nuttiness of whole grain flours. And although I'm not a vegan years later, I'm not surprised that the smell of cooked eggs can still sometimes nauseate me; that period of radical experimentation, of changing my diet and exploring new foods and flavors, was a defining point in the way I think about food, nutrition and cooking for myself. In fact, it's really where my entire cooking and baking journey began.

I hope you enjoy these recipes as much as I enjoyed reimagining them.

SIGHT: SHAPES, COLORS AND PATTERNS

I eat with my eyes before I eat with my tongue. That's where most anticipation builds. Seeing the shapes, colors, patterns and the way it all gets arranged on the plate or platter is so important to opening my appetite. Growing up, our family dinners lacked bright colors—although I doubt I could've worked up an appetite for green things back then anyhow; most things I ate stayed in the brown or beige category. And while I can still salivate over stews with gravy-thick sauces or piles of cheesy lasagnas disheveled and shoveled onto my plate, I've learned over time to crave an abundance of colors and textures. Yes, some phenomena, like neon-orange slices of cheese, can stop my appetite, but decadent and luscious things like dripping caramel and chocolate, or mesmerizing patterns like braided bread, will make it hard for me to stop staring.

OATMEAL CHEDDAR CHEESE MOON PIES

My daddy had curious cravings, some of them he's passed down to me, like his obsession for Raisinets, and others took time to grow on me—oatmeal cream pies with slices of cheddar cheese. He'd top a craggy pie with one of those plastic-wrapped squares of American cheese, and eat it like an open-faced sandwich. At the time, the sight of that neon cheddar on top was ghastly, but I see now, how for him, it was always about the marriage of the sweet and salty. I've followed his footsteps with this recipe, but not without toning down the menacing orange hue first. I'm using an all-natural white cheddar to help make this pairing much easier on the eyes.

EGG-FREE, WHOLE WHEAT
MAKES ABOUT 7 MOON PIES

OATMEAL COOKIES

1 cup (80 g) old-fashioned rolled oats

½ cup (112 g) softened unsalted butter

¾ cup (170 g) packed light brown sugar

2 tbsp (30 g) unsweetened applesauce, at room temperature

1 tsp vanilla extract

¾ cup + 2 tbsp (120 g) white whole wheat flour

1 tsp ground cinnamon

¼ tsp ground allspice

½ tsp baking soda

½ tsp salt

CHEDDAR CHEESE FILLING

8 oz (225 g) cream cheese, softened

4 oz (112 g) mild white cheddar, shredded

Preheat the oven to 350°F (180°C or gas mark 4) and have 2 parchment-lined sheet trays nearby.

To make the cookies, in a blender or food processor, pulse the rolled oats 20 times so that the oats are chopped and crumbly but not fine like flour. Set aside. In a large bowl or stand mixer, cream the softened butter and brown sugar together until fluffy. Add the applesauce and vanilla and beat again until fully incorporated.

In a separate bowl, mix together the flour, cinnamon, allspice, baking soda and salt. Fold the dry ingredients into the wet ingredients, and finally, fold in the pulsed oats. Drop about 1 heaping tablespoon (15 g) of batter onto the cookie sheets, leaving 2 to 3 inches (5 to 7.5 cm) between each cookie. Bake for 12 to 15 minutes, or until golden brown. Remove from the oven and allow to cool completely on a wire rack.

To make the filling, combine the cream cheese and cheddar in a bowl and melt slightly either over a double boiler or in the microwave just until the mixture is easy to spread. Fill the cooled cookies and serve.

ALTERNATIVE FILLING: Try a sweeter version by replacing the cheddar with 1 cup (120 g) of sifted confectioners' sugar.

(NOT AN) EASY BAKE CAKE WITH RASPBERRY GLAZE

I got as old as five before we moved from our first house on Chickashaw Lane. By then I had learned to read, chopped off all my hair against my daddy's will AND got my first Easy Bake Oven—a dream come true.

But my first exchange with the toy was dissatisfying at best. Fiddling with its cheap plastic timer and baby-size portions at a time in my life when I could really put it away, it was all so cruel. I'm remaking this chocolate cake so it's bigger, actually tastes good and has a real raspberry-pink icing. It makes up for lost times.

EGG-FREE, VEGAN OPTION, WHOLE WHEAT
MAKES ONE 9-INCH (23-CM) CAKE

CAKE

1¾ cups (210 g) white whole wheat flour

½ cup (60 g) cocoa powder

1 tsp baking soda

1 tsp baking powder

1 tsp salt

1 cup (225 g) packed light brown sugar

⅔ cup (160 g) yogurt, dairy-free if desired

¼ cup (60 g) unsweetened applesauce

¼ cup (60 ml) neutral oil or melted butter

2 tsp (10 ml) vanilla extract

1 cup (235 ml) hot brewed coffee

RASPBERRY GLAZE

1 cup (120 g) raspberries, rinsed

¼ cup (50 g) pure cane sugar or (60 ml) agave

Juice and zest of 1 lemon

½ cup (120 ml) melted coconut butter

Rainbow-colored star sprinkles, for topping (optional)

Preheat the oven to 350°F (180°C or gas mark 4) and have a 9-inch (23-cm) oiled cake pan lined with parchment nearby.

To make the cake, stir the flour, cocoa powder, baking soda, baking powder and salt together in a bowl. Set aside.

In a separate bowl, whisk the brown sugar, yogurt, applesauce, oil and vanilla extract together until smooth. Sift the dry ingredients into the wet ingredients, and fold them together gently to combine, being careful not to overmix. Then, pour in the hot coffee, and stir to combine. Pour the batter into the prepared cake pan and bake for 30 to 35 minutes, or until a toothpick inserted into the center comes out clean. Remove from the oven, allow to cool for 10 minutes, then turn the cake out onto a wire rack to finish cooling while you make the glaze.

To make the glaze, in a saucepan, combine the raspberries, cane sugar, lemon juice and lemon zest and cook, stirring occasionally, until the raspberries break down into a sauce, about 10 minutes. Remove the sauce from the heat and strain it through a sieve to remove the seeds. To the seedless sauce, stir in the coconut butter. Spread over the cooled, upside-down chocolate cake, and top with the sprinkles, if using. Slice and serve.

NOTES: For a more traditional icing, substitute the coconut butter with 1 to 2 cups (120 to 240 g) of confectioners' sugar.

BLUE BLUEBERRY DROP BISCUITS

There is something alarming about blue food. A real saturated blue feels artificial and my mind struggles to connect it to a flavor. I find it amusing to take something as welcoming and familiar as a warm buttermilk biscuit, the kind that would wake me on the occasional Sunday morning, and turn it blue.

30 MINUTES OR LESS, EGG-FREE, VEGAN OPTION, WHOLE WHEAT
MAKES 9 BISCUITS

½ cup (75 g) frozen wild blueberries

⅔ cup (160 ml) buttermilk, plus more for brushing

¼ cup (50 g) granulated sugar

1¾ cups (210 g) whole wheat pastry flour or unbleached all-purpose flour

2 tsp (5 g) baking powder

¼ tsp baking soda

1 tsp salt

½ cup (112 g) cold butter, cut into ½" (1.3-cm) cubes, plus more for serving

Sugar in the raw, for sprinkling (optional)

Preheat the oven to 425°F (220°C or gas mark 7), and have a lined baking sheet nearby.

In a small bowl, toss the blueberries with the buttermilk and granulated sugar and set aside long enough for the milk to change color and get cold, 5 to 10 minutes.

In a large mixing bowl, stir the flour, baking powder, baking soda and salt together. Toss in the cubes of butter and flatten them between your fingers, breaking them into the flour just enough until the flour becomes damp and slightly mealy but there are still chunks of chickpea-size butter cubes dispersed throughout the flour. Make a well in the center of the flour and add the blueberries and buttermilk, mixing gently with your hands, compressing just until it comes together into a dough. You may or may not need all the liquid.

Using a large ice cream scoop, drop about ¼-cup (60-g) spoonfuls of the batter onto the baking sheet, keeping 1 to 2 inches (2.5 to 5 cm) of space between each biscuit. Brush the tops with more buttermilk, sprinkle with the raw sugar, if you like, and bake for 12 to 15 minutes, or until puffed, golden on the outside and powder blue on the inside.

Remove from the oven, and serve warm with more butter.

NOTE: The longer you let the blueberries soak in the buttermilk, the bluer the biscuits get. Place the bowl in the fridge to keep cold while they soak.

VEGAN OPTION: Replace the butter with dairy-free butter and replace the buttermilk with ⅔ cup (160 ml) of nut or grain milk mixed with 1 teaspoon of lemon juice or apple cider vinegar. Let the mixture sit for 5 minutes to curdle before adding it to the recipe.

CHARCOAL BANANA BREAD

I usually wait until the skins of my bananas blacken to the color of charcoal before I finally commit to turning them into bread. That's when they make the kind of banana bread I go crazy for.

VEGAN, WHOLE WHEAT
MAKES ONE 9-INCH (23-CM) LOAF

3 very ripe bananas, blended into a puree

1 cup (235 ml) nut or grain milk

½ cup (120 ml) melted coconut oil or ½ cup (120 ml) neutral oil

1 cup (200 g) organic pure cane sugar or other granulated sugar

1 tbsp (15 ml) vanilla extract

2 cups (240 g) white whole wheat flour or spelt flour

1 tsp salt

2 tsp (5 g) baking powder

½ tsp baking soda

1 tsp activated food-grade charcoal powder, for color (optional)

¼ cup (40 g) cacao nibs, plus more for sprinkling (optional)

Preheat the oven to 400°F (200°C or gas mark 6) and position a rack in the upper middle of the oven. Spray a loaf pan with cooking spray and line it with a 4-inch (10-cm)-wide strip of parchment long enough to stretch across the width and up the sides with a little hanging over.

In a large bowl, whisk together the pureed banana, milk, coconut oil, sugar and vanilla until combined.

In a separate bowl, sift together the flour, salt, baking powder, baking soda and charcoal powder, if using, until combined. Add the dry ingredients into the bowl with the wet ingredients, along with the cacao nibs, if using, and fold until combined, being very careful not to overmix. Scoop the mixture into the oiled and lined loaf pan, and gently smooth out the top. Sprinkle with more cacao nibs, and bake in the oven for 30 to 40 minutes, or until a toothpick inserted into the center comes out clean.

Remove the bread from the oven, and let it rest for at least 20 minutes before lifting it from the pan. Transfer to a wire rack to cool for at least another 10 minutes, then slice and serve with nut butter or other favorite topping.

NOTE: Be careful to fold the wet and dry ingredients together gently and not overmix. Overmixing even slightly will make a dense crumb that is hard to cook through to the center.

OPTIONAL BANANA ICING: Blend 1 ripe banana with ½ cup (60 g) of confectioners' sugar. Drizzle over the warm banana bread. Slice and serve.

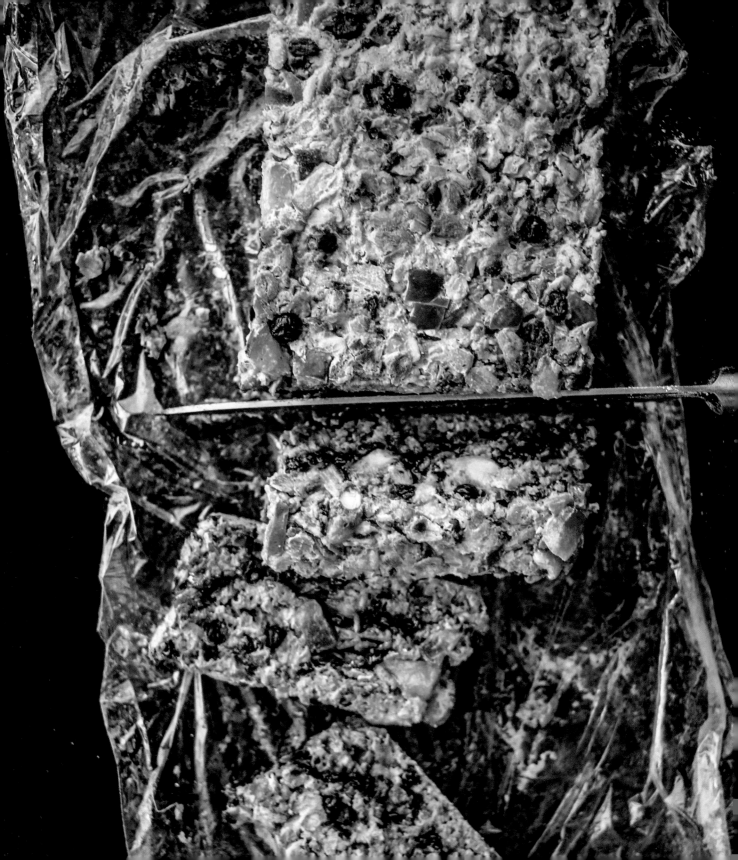

AMBROSIA BREAKFAST BREAD

My mother is not an earnest cook. For her, cooking should take 15 minutes or less and pair well with a bowl of steamed rice. So Christmas evenings, when it was time for her to bring a dish over to my granny's house, she'd reach for one of those 6-pound (2.7-kg) Del Monte cans of fruit cocktail drenched in syrup, drain the fruit, add it to a big bowl of sour cream and sugar, cover it with some plastic wrap and we'd be on our way. I've inherited a similar attitude toward some recipes that I make too often—overnight oats, for one. Granola—I can't be bothered to measure or tend to it.

This is an ugly one, just like ambrosia salad, but it tastes like breakfast parfait. This recipe is for the days you rebel against the kitchen and time spent overthinking.

EGG-FREE, GLUTEN-FREE, VEGAN OPTION
MAKES ONE 9-INCH (23-CM) LOAF

4 cups (480 g) gluten-free granola

2 cups (500 g) yogurt or coconut yogurt

1 cup (130 g) diced fresh fruit

Line a loaf pan with a couple sheets of plastic wrap and leave 3 to 4 inches (7.5 to 10 cm) hanging over around the edges.

In a large bowl, combine all the ingredients and dump the mixture into the loaf pan. Compress with the back of a spoon, fold the extra plastic wrap over the top to completely encase the mixture and leave in the fridge overnight. In the morning, remove the loaf from the pan, slice and serve.

NOTE: Sometimes when I only have regular unsweetened yogurt, I add a layer of my favorite jam to the middle of the bread. Just add half the mixture to the loaf pan, compress, spread 3 to 4 tablespoons (45 to 60 g) jam in the center, and then cover with the final layer.

IDEAS FOR FRUIT ADDITION (DRIED AND FRESH): Peaches, plums, mango, blueberries, green apples.

SEA SALT BUTTER-SCOTCH TART

While it cooks, watch as the coconut cream filling bubbles and reduces. The color will deepen to a gorgeous butterscotch, and as it cools the sauce will spill into smooth ribbons that'll make it hard for you to wait for the tart to set.

VEGAN, GLUTEN-FREE
MAKES ONE 9-INCH (23-CM) ROUND TART OR ONE 4 X 14-INCH (10 X 36-CM) TART

SHORTBREAD CRUST

¼ cup (56 g) virgin coconut oil, at room temperature, or softened butter

½ cup (100 g) granulated sugar

1 tsp vanilla extract

2 cups (240 g) almond meal flour

½ tsp salt

FILLING

½ cup (112 g) coconut oil or butter

⅔ cup (160 g) packed light brown sugar or coconut sugar

⅔ cup (160 ml) canned coconut cream

1 tsp kosher salt

Flaked sea salt, for sprinkling

Sliced Granny Smith apple, for topping (optional)

Preheat the oven to 375°F (190°C or gas mark 5) and have a 9-inch (23-cm) round tart pan or a 4 x 14-inch (10 x 36-cm) tart pan nearby.

To make the crust, in a bowl with a handheld mixer or a stand mixer with a paddle attachment, cream the coconut oil, granulated sugar and vanilla together until fluffy. Mix in the almond meal and salt. Then press the mixture evenly into the bottom and up the sides of the tart pan. Place the entire tart pan in the freezer for 10 minutes to harden, then bake in the oven for 15 minutes, or until the edges brown and the center is crusty. Remove from the oven and allow it to cool.

To make the filling, in a saucepan, combine the coconut oil, brown sugar, coconut cream and salt. Bring to a boil, and cook over medium heat for about 25 minutes. Have a cup of ice water nearby. Dip the tip of a fork into the boiling sugar and then into the ice water; if the sugar sticks between the tines of the fork without dissolving, the filling is ready. Pour it into the cooled tart pan, sprinkle with the sea salt, arrange sliced green apples on top, if desired, and let it cool for at least 30 minutes to harden before slicing and serving.

NOTE: Be sure to shake the can of coconut cream before measuring it, because it separates while it sits.

FUDGY FLOURLESS BROWNIE PIE

When I see deep fissures stretching across the surface of my brownie, and a gloss finish that looks like the top's been varnished with clear acrylic, I know those signs mean better texture. A crackled top with a dense fudge underneath makes the perfect brownie. Serve with raspberries and whipped cream, if you like.

GLUTEN-FREE
MAKES ONE 9-INCH (23-CM) PIE

BROWNIES

¾ cup (90 g) cacao powder, sifted

1 tsp espresso powder

¼ tsp baking soda

¾ tsp salt

1 cup (175 g) semisweet chocolate chips

13 tbsp (182 g) softened unsalted butter or coconut oil, divided

1 cup (200 g) sugar

2 tsp (10 ml) vanilla extract

4 eggs, at room temperature

TAHINI MAPLE SPREAD

¼ cup (60 g) tahini paste

¼ cup (60 ml) grade A maple syrup

1 tbsp (8 g) espresso powder

½ tsp salt

½ tsp vanilla extract

Preheat the oven to 375°F (190°C or gas mark 5) and have an oiled 9-inch (23-cm) springform pan or cake pan nearby.

To make the brownies, sift the cacao powder, espresso, baking soda and salt into a bowl and set aside. In the microwave or over a double boiler, melt the chocolate chips and 2 tablespoons (28 g) of the butter, stirring until the chocolate comes together into a thick fudge. Remove from the heat and set aside to cool.

In a stand mixer with a paddle attachment or with an electric mixer, cream together the sugar, vanilla and remaining 11 tablespoons (154 g) of butter until pale, scraping down the sides of the bowl and the beater as you go. Separate 3 of the eggs and add the egg yolks, one at a time, waiting until they are fully incorporated before adding another yolk, then add the whole egg and mix to combine.

Add 1 tablespoon (15 ml) of the cooled chocolate butter mixture at a time, continuing to beat after each addition until fully incorporated. Mix in the dry ingredients, beating until just combined.

In a separate clean metal bowl, beat the egg whites until soft peaks form, about 5 minutes. Make sure no bits of egg yolk sneak into the bowl, or the fat in the yolk won't allow the whites to lift while beating. Add the whipped egg whites to the batter in 3 additions, folding gently to keep the air in the whites from deflating. Once it's mostly combined (a few streaks of white is okay), pour the batter into the prepared baking pan. Bake for 45 minutes, or until the crust gets shiny and cracks, and a toothpick inserted into one of the cracks comes out clean. Transfer to a wire rack to cool slightly.

To make the tahini spread, combine the tahini paste, maple syrup, espresso powder, salt and vanilla in a blender or food processor and blend until completely smooth and creamy and almost all the granules of espresso are no longer visible. Serve alongside a slice of the brownie pie.

UNICORN ICE CREAM SANDWICHES

I've never let go of my obsession with ice cream sandwiches, the kind made of thin sheets of chocolate cake. The evolution of the way I took my ice cream between those two soft slabs of cake changed with phases. My basic vanilla stage lasted throughout my childhood. A few years after that I stepped up my game to Neapolitan. As a high school vegan, I could pound back two or three of the dairy-free kind I bought from the grocery store while I waited for a ride home. And now, I'm curious about the pastel pinks and blues littering my social feeds that seem to be so trendy. I agree, these creamy colors feel fantastical and airy, and give me a momentary escape from my everyday realities.

EGG-FREE, VEGAN OPTION
MAKES 12 ICE CREAM SANDWICHES

CAKE LAYER

1 cup (120 g) white whole wheat flour

¾ cup (90 g) cocoa powder

½ tsp salt

½ tsp baking soda

½ cup (112 g) unsalted dairy-free butter, softened

1 cup (225 g) packed brown sugar

1 tsp vanilla extract

½ cup (120 ml) flax egg (see page 30), at room temperature

½ cup (120 ml) nut or grain milk

Preheat the oven to 350°F (180°C or gas mark 4), and have two 9 x 13-inch (23 x 33-cm) rimmed sheet pans lined with pieces of parchment that are oiled and cut the same size as the bases of the pans.

To make the cake, in a medium bowl, sift together the flour, cocoa powder, salt and baking soda. Set aside.

In a bowl with an electric beater, cream together the butter, brown sugar and vanilla until fluffy, scraping down the sides of the bowl and beater as you go, about 3 minutes. Slowly drizzle in the flax egg, mixing until incorporated. On low speed, add the flour in three batches, alternating with the milk, just until incorporated. The batter will be thick and sticky. Divide the batter in half and drop dollops of it onto the oiled sheet pans. Spread it out to the edges of each pan. You can spray a sheet of parchment paper with cooking spray and place it sprayed-side down over the batter, to help press it into the shape of the pan—it makes for an easy, even layer.

Bake the sheet cakes for 12 to 15 minutes, or until browned and cooked through. Remove from the oven, allow to cool for 5 minutes and then turn the cakes out onto a wire rack to cool completely. Transfer to the freezer to harden slightly while you make the semifreddo.

(continued)

UNICORN ICE CREAM SAND- WICHES (CONT.)

Unicorn Semifreddo Filling

1 cup (235 ml) oat or nut milk

1 cup (200 g) granulated sugar, divided

2 tbsp (12 g) tapioca flour

2 tsp (10 ml) vanilla extract

¼ tsp salt

Natural red food powder

Natural purple food powder

Natural deep blue food powder

½ cup (120 ml) aquafaba*, at room temperature

½ tsp cream of tartar

2¼ cups (530 ml) heavy cream or 3 (15-oz [420-g]) cans chilled coconut cream with coconut water discarded, divided

To make the filling, in a saucepan over medium heat, combine the milk, half the granulated sugar, tapioca flour, vanilla and salt and stir occasionally until the mixture thickens, 5 to 7 minutes, never letting the liquid come to a full boil. Remove the mixture from the heat and divide it among 3 small bowls. To each bowl add a pinch of one of the powdered food colors, stirring and adding more until they're all vibrant colors. Cover the bowls with plastic wrap, and set them aside to cool completely.

Have 4 mixing bowls on hand. In one bowl, using a handheld beater, whip the aquafaba, remaining sugar and cream of tartar until stiff peaks are formed, about 5 minutes. Set aside.

Divide the heavy cream among the 3 bowls. Whip them all to soft peaks, then add one of the dyed milk mixtures to each bowl, and whip them each to stiff peaks, wiping down the beater after each one. To each bowl, carefully fold in one-third of the whipped aquafaba, being careful not to deflate them.

Remove the cakes from the freezer, unwrap one, resting it over a few sheets of plastic wrap. Dollop the colorful cream across the surface, alternating the colors. Swirl a butter knife through the cream to mix the colors, then place the other cake on top, pressing it down gently to help bring the filling to the edges. Fold the edges of the plastic wrap up and over the sandwich, adding another sheet on top if needed, and place the entire ice cream sandwich back on a sheet pan. Place it in the freezer to harden for 6 to 8 hours, or overnight.

Slice into bars the next day and serve. Or keep them in an airtight container in the freezer for at least 2 months.

FILLING ALTERNATIVE: Use vanilla ice cream or dairy-free vanilla ice cream.

MAKING FLAX EGGS: I always make large batches of flax eggs. I just stir together 1 cup (112 g) of golden flaxseed meal (my favorite brand is Bob's Red Mill) with 3 cups (705 ml) of warm water. I let the mixture sit for 20 minutes or up to overnight, and keep it covered in the fridge for up to a week, scooping from it as I need.

Aquafaba is the liquid brine from a can of chickpeas or legumes. A 15-ounce (420-g) can has about ¾ cup (176 ml) of aquafaba. Save the chickpeas or legumes and use them in a salad or other dish later on.

SUMMERTIME PAVLOVA POPS

Whipping egg whites became the splinter in my culinary side when I lived in Texas. My mother's friend from Australia brought her mango Pavlova to a housewarming party, and it was the first time I'd ever tasted anything like it. The marshmallow center. The crackling edges. The cold whipped cream on top. I went home to try and make some more to eat in solitude, but it was the summertime, and my meringue always fell flat. Or it burned, or it wept. A couple of years later, after moving to a snow city and putting myself through a dozen more tries, my eyes now know how to spot the silky white peaks I kept hearing about in cookbooks, and when to stop beating a bowl.

VEGAN
MAKES 6 POPS

EGG-FREE MERINGUE

⅔ cup (160 ml) aquafaba*

½ tsp cream of tartar

1¼ cups (250 g) superfine sugar

2 tbsp (16 g) arrowroot starch or cornstarch

1 tsp white vinegar

1 tsp vanilla extract

Pinch of salt

MANGO CURD

1 cup (225 g) mango or passion fruit puree

¼ cup (60 ml) lime juice (about 4 limes)

½ cup (100 g) granulated sugar

¼ cup (30 g) arrowroot starch or cornstarch

2–3 tbsp (30–45 ml) cold water

Preheat the oven to 275°F (125°C or gas mark 1) and position a rack in the center of the oven. Have a half baking sheet lined with parchment nearby.

To make the meringue, in a large clean metal bowl with a handheld mixer or in the bowl of a stand mixer with the whisk attachment, add the aquafaba and cream of tartar and beat on high speed until they become frothy and then soft peaks begin to form, about 2 minutes. Slowly add the superfine sugar, 1 tablespoon (12 g) at a time, beating until the liquid turns stiff, 6 to 7 minutes. With the beater still running, add in the arrowroot starch, vinegar, vanilla and salt until it looks like stiff marshmallow creme.

Using a spoon or an offset spatula, spoon the meringue onto the baking sheet, in 6 rough 2 x 4-inch (5 x 10-cm) rectangles that are 1 to 2 inches (2.5 to 5 cm) tall. They will spread, so use another baking sheet if you can't fit them all. Carefully insert a wide Popsicle stick through the bottom and into the center of the meringue, cover the sticks with a little more of the meringue mixture just to make sure the sticks are secure and then bake them for 30 to 35 minutes, or until they've cracked and hardened. Turn off the oven and let the meringue sit to cool to room temperature, about 1 hour. Remove from the oven and allow them to cool completely before adding the toppings.

To make the curd, in a saucepan, combine the pureed mango, lime juice and granulated sugar and cook, stirring constantly, until the sugar dissolves, about 3 minutes. In a small bowl, mix the arrowroot starch with the cold water until smooth, and add it to the saucepan, stirring constantly until it thickens. Transfer the mixture to a bowl, and press a sheet of plastic directly over the surface. Keep in the fridge to chill.

(continued)

SUMMER-TIME PAVLOVA POPS (CONT.)

To make the whipped coconut cream, open the cans upside down and drain away the coconut water that has separated from the cream. Scoop out the coconut cream and add to a bowl along with the agave, if using, and vanilla. Beat until whipped, about 3 to 4 mintues.

When ready to serve, spoon the chilled mango curd and whipped coconut cream over the tops of the meringue pops.

NOTE: If you can't find superfine sugar, just process granulated sugar in a food processor until it turns fluffy, about 3 minutes.

---

* Aquafaba is the liquid brine from a can of chickpeas or legumes. A 15-ounce (420-g) can has about ¾ cup (175 ml) of aquafaba. Save the chickpeas or legumes and use them in a salad or other dish later on.

WHIPPED COCONUT CREAM

2 (15-oz [420-g]) cans chilled coconut cream

2 tbsp (30 ml) agave or other sweetener (optional)

2 tsp (10 ml) vanilla extract

Fresh summer berries, for serving (optional)

BUTTER PECAN BUNDT CAKE

I love staring at the curves of a Bundt cake. I guess it's the way the pan holds and distributes heat that makes these cakes turn out so moist and tender. Slowly drizzling a silky glaze or caramel sauce over the top and watching it inch down the edges and arches, making the cake glisten, is so sensual. I can't help but stare.

VEGAN, WHOLE WHEAT
MAKES ONE 9-INCH (23-CM) BUNDT CAKE

BUNDT CAKE

1 cup (145 g) chopped pecans halves

2½ cups (300 g) white whole wheat flour

4 tsp (12 g) baking powder

1 tsp salt

1 cup (235 ml) oat or nut milk, at room temperature

1 tbsp (15 ml) apple cider vinegar or lemon juice

1 cup (225 g) softened unsalted, dairy-free butter

1 cup (200 g) pure cane sugar

1 tbsp (15 ml) vanilla extract

1 tsp rum (optional)

½ cup (120 g) applesauce, at room temperature

PECAN GLAZE

½ cup (120 ml) maple syrup

1 cup (225 g) muscovado or packed brown sugar

½ cup (120 ml) oat or nut milk

1 tbsp (15 ml) rum

1 tbsp (15 ml) vanilla extract

1 tsp salt

Preheat the oven to 350°F (180°C or gas mark 4). Oil a 9-inch (23-cm) Bundt cake pan with cooking spray and set aside.

To make the cake, toast the pecans by spreading them out on a sheet pan and baking them for 8 to 10 minutes, or until browned. Remove from the oven and set them aside to cool until it's time to make the pecan glaze.

In a large bowl, combine the flour, baking powder and salt and set aside.

In a small bowl, combine the milk and apple cider vinegar. Set it aside to curdle, about 5 minutes.

In a large bowl with a hand mixer or in a stand mixer with a paddle attachment, cream the butter and sugar together until fluffy, about 3 minutes, scraping down the sides of the bowl and beater as you go. Add the vanilla and rum, if using. Slowly add the applesauce, beating on medium-high speed, until the applesauce is completely mixed in. Turn the speed to low and add the flour mixture in batches, alternating with the milk and vinegar mixture, until everything is just combined. Pour the batter into the oiled Bundt pan, and bake for 25 to 30 minutes, or until a toothpick comes out clean. Allow it to cool slightly for 5 minutes, then carefully turn it out onto a serving tray while you make the glaze.

To make the glaze, in a small saucepan, combine the maple syrup, muscovado, milk, rum, vanilla and salt and bring to a boil, then reduce the heat to medium and allow it to cook until it's reduced by half, about 10 minutes. Add the toasted nuts, stirring to combine, then remove the sauce from the heat. Allow it to cool slightly so it thickens, then pour it over the cake when you're ready to serve.

RINGLET BAGELS

The process of coiling this dough and wrapping it around a thin metal rod helps create the tightest curls. I tug them and watch them spring back into place—like the curls I used to wear as a little girl—but they also make breakfast more portable. I just pipe whipped cream cheese into the center and go about my day.

EGG-FREE, DAIRY-FREE
MAKES 12–15 BAGELS

BAGEL DOUGH

1¼ cups (295 ml) warm water

2 tbsp (25 g) packed brown sugar

1 (2½-tsp [9-g]) packet active dry yeast

3 cups + 2 tbsp (276 g) flour

1 tsp salt

TOPPINGS

Black or white sesame seeds, caraway seeds, onion flakes, dried garlic flakes, flaky sea salt, poppy seeds, OR
1 cup (200 g) granulated sugar plus 1 tbsp (8 g) ground cinnamon

Your favorite bagel spread, for serving

NOTE: If you don't have mini cannoli rods, you can use the end of a wooden spoon.

STORING: These bagels should be kept in an airtight bag right after baking. Their thin body means they'll get stale too quickly if they're left on the countertop. They can be kept in the freezer, too.

To make the dough, add the warm water to a bowl along with the brown sugar. Sprinkle the yeast over the top of the water, and let it sit and bloom without mixing until a thick cap of froth is formed, 5 to 10 minutes.

In a stand mixer with a dough hook attachment, add the flour and salt, and mix. Dump in the bloomed yeast and knead for 5 to 6 minutes, adding more warm water or flour if needed to pull it together. The dough should be very dense and heavy with no visible traces of flour. Cover with plastic wrap and a damp cloth and let rise in a warm place for 1 hour, or until doubled in size.

Have a couple baking sheets lined with parchment nearby. Punch the risen dough down with your fist to allow the extra air to escape, and then separate the dough into 2-inch (5-cm) pieces. Roll the dough between your palms until a firm, smooth ball is formed, then roll the ball into a short coil. On a clean work surface, roll the small coil into a 10-inch (25-cm) coil. It's best if you don't add flour in this step because a damper dough will stick to the work surface better, making it easier to roll. Transfer the coils of dough to the lined baking sheets, cover with plastic wrap and let them rise and rest for another 30 minutes.

Preheat the oven to 425°F (220°C or gas mark 7) and have at least 3 lightly oiled mini cannoli rods and a lined and lightly oiled baking sheet nearby.

Bring a large pot of water to a boil and then reduce the heat to a simmer. Remove the plastic wrap from the dough, and begin wrapping them around metal cannoli rods, pinching the edges so they don't unravel in the water. You can do this in batches, being sure to cover up the dough not being used so it doesn't develop a hard crust.

Drop the bagels into the hot water, and as soon as they float to the top, about 1 minute, scoop them out using a spider or a slotted spoon. Place on the baking sheet, and while they're still wet, sprinkle them with the toppings so they stick. Once all the twirls are boiled and seasoned, bake in the oven for 10 minutes, or until golden brown. Serve warm with your bagel spread either as a dip on the side or piped into the center.

EVERYTHING CHICKPEA TURMERIC CRACKERS

Something about the color of chickpea flour seems timid. It's a pale yellow that is in desperate need of some color saturation. I've found that a good heaping of turmeric helps the color measure up to the vibrant flavor of these curried pita chips.

20 MINUTES OR LESS, GLUTEN-FREE, VEGAN
MAKES 2–3 CUPS (300–450 G) CRACKERS

TOPPING

2 tsp (8 g) poppy seeds

2 tsp (5 g) black sesame seeds

2 tsp (4 g) caraway seeds

½ tsp salt

CRACKERS

2 cups (240 g) chickpea flour, plus more for dusting

2 tsp (5 g) turmeric

1 tsp ground cumin

1 tsp garlic powder

1 tsp onion powder

½ tsp salt

2 tbsp (30 ml) olive oil, plus more for drizzling

6 tbsp (90 ml) water

Preheat the oven to 425°F (220°C or gas mark 7), position a rack in the center of the oven and have a lightly oiled sheet tray nearby.

To make the topping, in a small bowl, mix together the poppy seeds, sesame seeds, caraway seeds and salt. Set aside.

To make the crackers, in a mixing bowl, combine the chickpea flour, turmeric, cumin, garlic powder, onion powder and salt. Then add the olive oil, and toss to disperse. Add the water, 2 tablespoons (30 ml) at a time, tossing and compressing the mixture gently to bring it all together; you may not need all of the water. Form the dough into a disk and roll the disk out between two sheets of parchment paper until it's about ⅛-inch (3-mm) thick. Remove the top parchment, cut the dough into your preferred cracker shapes and then transfer them to the baking sheet. Drizzle them lightly with more olive oil, and sprinkle them with the topping mixture. Bake for 5 to 6 minutes, or until golden brown and crispy. Remove from the oven and allow to cool completely. Serve with cream cheese or your favorite dip.

HIDDEN HERB GARLIC KNOTS

It wasn't usual for us to cook with fresh herbs. Garnishes that, in the words of my big brother, "looked like weeds plucked from outside," were impractical, and didn't come included in the boxes of Stouffer's frozen dinners we loved. But then, during a time when I was old enough to cook the family dinners, I stumbled on a produce market tucked behind the landscaping lot on Hypoluxo Lane, and discovered I could buy bouquets of parsley, sweet-smelling basil, rosemary and lemon-scented thyme for fractions of a dollar. And then for a period after that, everything that was a family staple—biscuits, garlic breads, grits—got sheathed in a sprinklage of my favorite fresh and fragrant herbs. A lot of times my dad or brother would object, so I would just be sure to do a better job of hiding them . . .

VEGAN OPTION
MAKES ABOUT 8 KNOTS

DOUGH

¾ cup (180 ml) warm water

3 tbsp (36 g) packed brown sugar or granulated sugar

1½ tsp (5 g) active dry yeast

2 cups (240 g) unbleached all-purpose flour

½ tsp salt

2 tbsp (30 ml) olive oil

HERB FILLING

¾ cup (45 g) packed roughly chopped fresh parsley

2 tbsp (2 g) roughly chopped chives

7–8 large leaves fresh basil

4 sprigs of fresh oregano

2 sprigs of fresh rosemary

5 cloves garlic

1 tbsp (15 ml) olive oil

GARLIC BUTTER

2 tbsp (30 ml) melted butter (dairy-free, if desired)

2 cloves garlic, minced

1 tsp flaky sea salt

To make the dough, add the water and brown sugar to a small bowl. Sprinkle over the yeast, and let it bloom until a cap of froth forms on the top, 5 to 10 minutes.

In a stand mixer with a dough hook attachment, stir together the flour and salt. Add the bloomed yeast to the bowl along with the olive oil. Knead the dough for 5 minutes. Cut the dough into 1-inch (2.5-cm) pieces and knead them into balls between your palms for about 1 minute, pressing firmly to work out all the crinkles and crags. Place the balls on an oiled cookie sheet, tossing them in the oil to coat, cover the pan loosely with plastic wrap and leave in a warm dry place to double in size, about 1 hour.

To make the herb filling, combine all the herbs, garlic and olive oil in a food processor or blender and blend until uniform, removing any tough stems or leaves that won't blend. Set aside. Have an oiled muffin tin nearby.

Once the balls have risen, remove the plastic wrap, flatten the balls and fold each piece over on itself 2 to 3 times. Fill the dough with ¼ to ½ teaspoon of the herb filling, and then pinch them sealed, placing seam-side down in the oiled muffin tin. Continue doing this, filling each muffin hole with 4 to 6 balls. Cover the assembled balls with plastic wrap and let the dough rest and rise for a final 30 minutes.

Preheat the oven to 375°F (190°C or gas mark 5), and position a rack in the center of the oven.

Remove the plastic from the dough. For the garlic butter, drizzle the melted butter over the tops of the buns, then sprinkle over the minced garlic and flaky sea salt. Bake the knots for 20 to 25 minutes, or until golden brown and slightly crusty on top. Remove from the oven and serve warm with a plate of spaghetti or something else delicious.

BAKED BUTTERMILK BEIGNETS

My daddy met a baker from New Orleans who wrote him a secret beignet recipe on the back of a napkin to pass along to me. My daddy took a picture of it with his phone and sent it to me, but I lost it. Years later, I wish I could tell you my photographic memory was better, but the reality is I'm forced to rely on my memories of mouthfeel and taste to guide me back to visits to the French Quarter.

VEGAN OPTION
MAKES 24 BEIGNETS

1 cup (235 ml) buttermilk, warmed to 115°F (46°C)

¼ cup (50 g) granulated sugar

2 tsp (7 g) active dry yeast

1 cup (120 g) white whole wheat flour

1¼–1½ cups (150–180 g) unbleached all-purpose flour, plus more for rolling

1 tsp salt

¼ cup (32 g) flax egg

4 tbsp (56 g) softened butter, plus more for oiling

Lots of confectioners' sugar, for serving

VEGAN OPTION: Make dairy-free buttermilk by combining 1 cup (235 ml) of thick plant-based milk with 1 tablespoon (15 ml) of lemon juice or apple cider vinegar. Replace the butter with dairy-free butter or softened virgin coconut oil.

Add the warm buttermilk and granulated sugar to a bowl. Sprinkle the yeast over the top. Allow the yeast to bloom until a thick cap of foam forms on top, 5 to 10 minutes.

In a large bowl or stand mixer with a dough hook attachment, stir together the flours and salt. Add the bloomed yeast mixture and flax egg and knead on medium-low speed until a shaggy dough is formed. Add the softened butter, and knead until a sticky dough forms and it starts to stick on the bottom of the mixer but not the sides, 5 to 6 minutes. It should be tacky but not wet. Add more flour if you need to. Place the dough in a well-oiled bowl, cover with plastic wrap and keep in a warm place to double in size, 60 to 90 minutes.

Have 2 lined half sheet pans on hand. Unwrap the dough, punch it down in the center to release the air, and roll it out on a lightly floured surface with a lightly floured rolling pin until it's ¾-inch (2-cm) thick. Cut the dough into 24 squares. Fold each square over on itself 5 times, covering the rest of the dough with plastic wrap while you work. Place the folded dough back on the baking sheet, cover with plastic wrap and let rest rise for another 45 to 60 minutes.

Preheat the oven to 375°F (190°C or gas mark 5) and position 2 racks in the center of the oven.

Unwrap the risen dough, and bake the beignets in the oven for 18 to 20 minutes, or until puffed and golden brown. Remove from the oven and dust with confectioners' sugar.

NOTE: I love to keep a small paper bag nearby and add my confectioners' sugar to the bag, then throw in 2 to 3 beignets, and shake vigorously to coat. Then serve. This is the way it's traditionally done.

PLAITED DUKKAH BREAD

It's easy to find parallels between breaded bread and braided hair. Whenever I see the swoops and curves of a rope of dough tightly knotting and hugging the other, I'm immediately brought back to afternoons of having my scalp split with the pointed handle of an orange-toothed comb. My tangled hair, snatched apart like treetops in a forest, combed, and somehow, after hours of patience and pain, masterfully tightened to my skull into a glorious, patterned coil.

MAKES ONE 16-INCH (40.6-CM) LOAF
VEGAN, WHOLE WHEAT

BREAD

¼ cup (32 g) flax meal

1½ cups (355 ml) warm water, divided

1 cup (225 g) packed brown sugar, divided

1 (2¼-tsp [9-g]) packet active dry yeast

2¼ cups (270 g) whole wheat pastry flour

3 cups (360 g) white whole wheat flour, plus more for dusting (I used an extra ¼ cup [30 g])

1 tsp salt

½ cup (120 ml) neutral oil

DUKKAH TOPPING

2 tbsp (14 g) chopped hazelnuts

2 tbsp (16 g) black or white sesame seeds

1 tsp ground cumin

1 tsp coriander seeds

Olive oil, for brushing

To make the bread, in a small bowl, stir together the flax meal and ¾ cup (180 ml) of the warm water, and set aside for 10 to 15 minutes until it becomes a slurry. Add the remaining ¾ cup (180 ml) of warm water to a bowl along with a couple tablespoons (25 g) of the brown sugar. Sprinkle the yeast over the top of the water, and let it sit and bloom until a thick cap of froth is formed, 5 to 10 minutes.

In a stand mixer with a dough hook attachment, mix the flours and salt. Add the remaining brown sugar, the bloomed yeast, the flax slurry and the oil, and then knead for 6 to 8 minutes, or until a dense and slightly sticky ball is formed around and starts inching up the dough hook. Add a few pinches of white whole wheat flour here and there if the dough is unbearably sticky. It's easier to handle the sticky dough with damp hands. Place the dough in a clean oiled bowl, cover it with plastic wrap or a damp kitchen towel and let it rise in a warm place for 60 to 90 minutes, or until doubled in size.

Have a lined half sheet pan nearby. Punch the risen dough down with your fist to allow the extra air to escape, and then separate the dough into 9 or 12 equal pieces, depending on the pattern you want to make. Roll the pieces into loose balls, then fold them on themselves 3 times. Roll them out into long, ¼-inch (6-mm)-thick ropes, and then line the ropes up next to each other on the baking sheet. Wrap the top ends of 3 of the ropes together, and then tuck them under themselves to make sure they don't unravel. Then, braid them together like you would strands of hair, tucking the ends together when you arrive at the end (see photo page 12). Repeat with the other ropes so you have 3 or 4 braided breads, then braid 3 breads together to make one large braid, tucking the ends under to keep the braids from unraveling. If you make a fourth braid, wrap it around the loaf for extra reinforcement. Cover the bread with plastic wrap and let it rise again for another 60 minutes, or until it's doubled in size. Don't let it grow larger than this.

Preheat the oven to 350°F (180°C or gas mark 4). To make the topping, combine the hazelnuts, sesame seeds, cumin and coriander seeds in a small bowl. Uncover the bread and brush the top gently with olive oil. Sprinkle on the topping and bake for 25 to 30 minutes, or until the bread turns golden brown on top and is cooked through. Remove from the oven and let the bread cool to room temperature before slicing and serving.

DOMINO DATE AND APPLE HAND PIES

My mom was obsessed with ordering those hand pies from the McDonald's drive-thru. She'd tip the box—which had these menacing ½-inch (1.3-cm) holes punched out the sides as if there were a breathing animal inside—and let the pie slide out and into her palm. Then she'd split it in half to share with me, and only me. It was always piping hot, its crust a little leathery from sitting under the lamp so long, but it was still delicious. They could've also dared to be a little bigger to support those apple chunks inside, but I loved its shape and flavor—everything else I am fine with tweaking.

VEGAN, WHOLE WHEAT
MAKES 6 HAND PIES

CRUST

2½ cups (300 g) whole wheat pastry flour

1 tbsp (12 g) sugar

1 tsp ground cinnamon

½ tsp salt

¾ cup (168 g) very cold unsalted dairy-free butter

½ cup + 2 tbsp (150 ml) ice cold water

2 tbsp (30 ml) apple cider vinegar

APPLE DATE FILLING

14 or 15 (253 g) Medjool dates, pitted and soaked to soften, then pureed into a paste

½ cup (125 g) unsweetened applesauce

3 tbsp (43 g) coconut oil

1 tsp ground cinnamon

¼ tsp allspice

1 tsp salt

3 Granny Smith apples (556 g), cored, peeled and shredded

Coconut yogurt, or other yogurt, for browning (optional)

To make the crust, in a large mixing bowl, combine the flour, sugar, cinnamon and salt, and stir to combine. Toss in the cubes of cold butter to coat. Using your thumb and index finger, squish the pieces of butter to flatten, and continue to break the butter up until 50 percent of the butter is crumbly, but not completely uniform in texture; you want there to be chickpea-size nuggets of butter still present. Stir together the water and vinegar, and then add it slowly to the flour mixture, mixing and gathering and compressing the flour with your hands until a shaggy dough is formed. You may not need all the liquid. Shape the dough into a disk, wrap in plastic wrap and refrigerate for at least 30 minutes. While the dough is chilling, prepare the filling.

To make the filling, in a small saucepan, combine the date paste, applesauce, coconut oil, cinnamon, allspice and salt, and bring to a boil. Cook for 5 minutes, or until the sauce is thick and smooth. Add the shredded apples and stir to combine, then remove from the heat to cool slightly.

Preheat the oven to 400°F (200°C or gas mark 6) and have a baking sheet lined with parchment nearby.

Once the dough is chilled, roll it out on a lightly floured surface into an ⅛-inch (3-mm)-thick rectangle. Trim the edges to make them even and then cut the dough into 12 equal rectangles, rolling out the dough a second time if you need.

Using the end of a metal piping tip, cut a few small steam holes out of 6 of the rectangles. Divide the cooled apple filling among the other 6 rectangles, then carefully top them with the piece of dough with holes punched out. Pinch and twist the edges closed, or crimp with a fork, carefully transfer them to the lined baking sheet and brush the tops with yogurt, if using. Bake for 30 minutes, or until golden brown on top. Remove from the oven and allow to cool slightly. Serve warm.

AROMA: SCENTS AND CINNAMON

My nose has given me a handful of some of my most vivid food memories. Some are unpleasant, like all the times I'd cut open a ripe papaya and get a funky smell that would make my nose hairs crimp. Or when I could smell granola burning in the oven, or got a whiff of the gamey smell of bloomed gelatin right before I chugged a cup of Jell-O. But other good smells have made up for them, like when I brown butter on the stove. You'll see, when you make my Macadamia Brown Butter Cashew Cookie Dough (page 62). It'll smell—and taste—like caramel. Then there's my nostalgia for cinnamon-scented foods. It was the only dessert spice we kept in the cabinet when I was younger, so my fascination with it is never-ending, and it always brings me back to Christmas mornings when we'd fry batches of rum-soaked French toast or huddle around to separate a jumble of cinnamon-sugar-coated dough balls we baked into an impressive loaf. Even now, I still pause in the bulk section of the supermarket, near the bins of granola, to savor all the ways they've managed to make cinnamon and oats smell like heaven. I didn't stumble on other aromatic spices like cardamom and clove until I moved away and started baking on my own. Now these spices and their smells have become indispensable, too.

HONEY WHEAT CINNAMON RAISIN BREAD

My daddy loved toasting slices of cinnamon raisin bread and slathering them with jam and butter to eat alongside his dinner. He almost always had honey wheat on hand, too, for workdays when he'd pack savory sandwiches, always needing a tinge of sweetness to round out the salt from the sliced turkey. I've combined the two breads here. I appreciate the floral sweetness the honey adds, and I love seeing the raisins bloat from the bourbon and hot milk and later char when baked. But really, my fascination with this recipe comes during the final stage, when the warmed cinnamon, sweet raisins and yeast caramelize under the broiler, perfuming the kitchen. The combination of those smells reminds me of him and being back home. Warning: I go heavy on the ground cinnamon here.

DAIRY-FREE, EGG-FREE
MAKES TWO 8-INCH (20.4-CM) LOAVES

DOUGH

3 tbsp (24 g) ground flaxseeds

½ cup (120 ml) warm water

1¼ cups (295 ml) nut or grain milk

¾ cup (113 g) raisins

1 tbsp (15 ml) bourbon (optional)

½ cup (119 ml) honey

1 (2½-tsp [9-g]) packet active dry yeast

2 cups (240 g) white whole wheat flour

2¾ cups (330 g) unbleached all-purpose flour, plus more for dusting

1 tsp coarse sea salt

4 tbsp (56 g) softened dairy-free butter, or virgin coconut oil

CINNAMON SUGAR FILLING

6 tbsp (84 g) softened dairy-free butter, or virgin coconut oil

¾ cup (150 g) sugar

2 tbsp (30 ml) milk

3 tbsp (23 g) ground cinnamon

To make the dough, in a small bowl, stir the ground flaxseeds into the warm water. Let it sit for at least 15 minutes to thicken.

Add the milk to a saucepan, and heat on the stove over low heat until it reaches around 125°F (52°C), but don't let it boil. Remove from the heat, and pour half the milk into a small bowl. Add the raisins and bourbon, if using, to the remaining milk and set aside to plump. To the bowl with the warm milk, add the honey and let it sink to the bottom. Sprinkle the yeast over the top; wait for the yeast to bloom and a cap of froth to form on the top, 5 to 10 minutes.

Stir the bloomed yeast and add it to a stand mixer with a dough hook attachment, along with the flours, salt, flax egg, and plumped raisins with milk. Knead on low speed, scraping down the sides of the bowl and hook as you go. Just as a ball begins to form, add the softened butter and continue to knead until smooth. Turn the speed up to medium and knead for 4 to 6 minutes. The dough should be sticky and pull away from the sides of the bowl but stick to the bottom of the bowl. Place the dough in a large, clean oiled bowl, flipping it over to coat. Cover the bowl with a warm, damp cloth and keep in a warm place to rise until doubled in size, about 1 hour and 40 minutes.

To make the filling, pulse together the butter, sugar, milk and cinnamon in a food processor until a thick paste is formed. You can also mix it together by hand, but the food processor makes for a smoother paste.

Pry the risen dough from the bottom of the bowl. Punch the dough down and dump it out onto a lightly floured surface. Lightly dust your hands, rolling pin and the top of the dough with more flour. Poke the dough lightly all round the surface with your fingertips, to help more of the air escape.

(continued)

HONEY WHEAT CINNAMON RAISIN BREAD (CONT.)

Gently stretch or roll it out to roughly 10 x 24 inches (25.4 x 60.7 cm). Spread the cinnamon sugar paste evenly on the dough. Tightly roll the dough into a log from the shorter end, slice the log in half and transfer them to two 8-inch (20.4-cm) oiled loaf tins, compressing the rolls slightly, like accordions, or folding the ends under to fit. Cover again with a warm damp rag and place in a warm dry place to double in size again, about another 1½ hours. The bread should peak out just slightly above the edges of the pan, or at least come up very close, but not mushroom over the top.

Preheat the oven to 350°F (180°C or gas mark 4), and position an oven rack on the lower half of the oven.

Bake the loaves for 50 minutes to 1 hour, or until you can hear a hollow knock when you tap on the bottom of the baked loaf with your knuckle. Transfer to a wire rack to cool for 20 minutes. Slice and serve.

TIP: If freezing, slice the loaf beforehand and toast slices as you crave them.

KNEADING BY HAND: The dough might originally be clumpy, but mound it up and press the base of your palm into the center of the dough, rolling it away from you and then folding the extended piece back over itself. Continue to do this, adding more flour if it sticks to the surface or your fingers, until the dough is smooth. This should take 1 to 2 minutes of kneading. Turn the dough out onto a lightly floured surface and continue to knead just until the dough feels tacky but doesn't stick to your fingers. You can add just a little more flour if it's unbearably sticky, but less flour means a more tender bread. Oil a clean bowl, add the dough to the bowl, flip over to coat the dough completely in oil and cover with a warm, damp cloth. Keep in a warm place to rise until doubled in size, about 1 hour 40 minutes.

PECAN PIE RUGELACH

I've acquired the new skill of being able to walk into any pastry shop in Boston and call out a batch of rugelach baking in the oven. I can recognize that unmistakable perfume of roasting berries and the cream cheese and butter melding into magic under the heat. The day I moved into my Boston apartment, my parents brought over a large container of these pie cookies to help me settle in. I had no idea what they were at the time. I fantasized about what their pie crust shells would be like stuffed with a bourbon pecan pie filling, the flavor of pie I used to inhale with no shame when I still lived in Texas.

EGG-FREE, WHOLE WHEAT, VEGAN OPTION
MAKES 24 COOKIES

RUGELACH CRUST

2½ cups (300 g) whole wheat pastry flour, plus more for dusting

1½ tsp (8 g) salt

¾ cup (168 g) cold unsalted butter

4 oz (112 g) cold cream cheese, cut into ½" (1.3-cm) chunks

2 tbsp (30 ml) bourbon or apple cider vinegar

1 tbsp (15 ml) vanilla extract

6 tbsp (90 ml) ice cold water

PECAN PIE FILLING

1 cup (145 g) pecan pieces

1 cup (225 g) packed brown sugar or coconut sugar

4 tbsp (56 g) butter or coconut oil

2 tbsp (30 ml) maple syrup

2 tbsp (30 ml) bourbon

2 tsp (10 ml) vanilla extract

1 tsp salt

¼ tsp cayenne pepper (optional)

To make the crust, combine the flour and salt together in a bowl. Cut the cold butter and cream cheese into the flour with the back of a fork or pastry blender until the flour is crumbly. In a separate small bowl, combine the bourbon, vanilla and water, and then add it to the flour mixture, a couple of tablespoons (30 ml) at a time, tossing and compressing the mixture gently with your hands until it forms a ball, being careful not to overwork the dough. Divide the dough in half and shape each half into a disk. Wrap each disk in plastic wrap and refrigerate for at least 2 hours, or overnight.

Preheat the oven to 375°F (190°C or gas mark 5) and line a baking sheet with parchment.

To make the filling, spread the pecans on the lined baking sheet and bake for 10 to 12 minutes, or until the nuts begin to perfume. Remove the nuts from the oven and pulse the nuts in a blender or food processor until it's mealy but not flour. Set aside.

In a saucepan, whisk the brown sugar, butter, maple syrup, bourbon, vanilla and salt together and cook over medium-high heat, stirring occasionally, until the liquid thickens and starts to look like the foam on a beer head, and you can see the bottom of the pan for a split second when you mix it, about 4 to 6 minutes. Remove the pan from the heat and add in the ground pecans and cayenne, if using. Allow the mixture to cool completely.

When the dough has chilled and the nuts and sugar have cooled and hardened, preheat the oven to 375°F (190°C or gas mark 5), and line 2 baking sheets with parchment.

(continued)

PECAN PIE RUGELACH (CONT.)

Remove the chilled dough from the fridge, unwrap, and, using a dusted rolling pin, roll it out into a ⅛-inch (3-mm)-thick rectangle about 15 x 8 inches (38 x 20 cm) on a lightly floured surface. Sprinkle half of the nut mixture evenly over the dough, taking the filling all the way to the edges. Starting on the longer end of the dough, roll the dough into a log and then cut into 12 equal pieces. Place the pieces on the baking sheet seam-side down and then place in the freezer while you do the same with the other half of the dough and filling mixture. Freeze the rugelach for 10 or so minutes before baking them in the oven. Bake for 20 to 25 minutes, or until the crust is golden and flaky. Transfer to a wire rack to cool for 10 minutes before serving.

VEGAN OPTION: Replace the butter in the crust with equal parts dairy-free butter or ½ cup (112 g) of cold coconut oil.

NOTE: You can also make the crust in a food processor. Just pulse the dry ingredients with the cream cheese and butter until the fat is the size of chickpeas. Then add the bourbon and vanilla and pulse just until a dough is formed and it starts to peel away from the edges of the bowl. Usually the crust has an egg yolk, but I make this one closer to the way I make regular pie dough, with butter and apple cider vinegar, so the proteins in the flour don't form long strands of gluten.

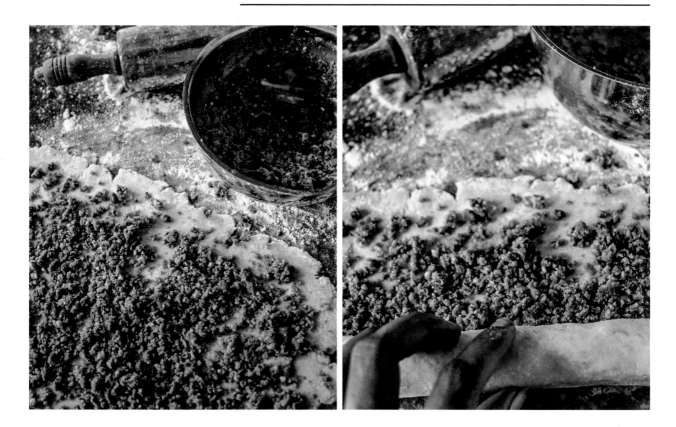

CASHEW CREAM STUFFED FRENCH TOAST

There wasn't anything special to me about French toast until I started getting more creative with the bread, stuffing it with cream and fruit, stacking it, rolling it out—that, and using lots of deep-flavored alcohol in the batter. One time I cracked open a pocket shot of Captain Morgan and dumped the whole thing in. When the bread hit the hot browning butter, I smelled the alcohol that had seeped into the bread's pores evaporate from the heat of the pan and waft up into my nostrils. It's my favorite thing to do to take boring French toast over the top.

DAIRY-FREE
MAKES 4 STUFFED FRENCH TOAST

CASHEW CREAM FILLING

2 cups (300 g) raw cashews

Zest and juice of 1 large lemon

2 tbsp (30 ml) maple syrup

¼ cup (60 ml) water

6 tbsp (75 g) coconut sugar, packed brown sugar or granulated sugar

BATTER

1½ cups (355 ml) oat or nut milk

3 large brown eggs

1 tsp vanilla extract

2 tsp (10 ml) rum

¼ cup (50 g) granulated sugar

12 slices bread (I use honey wheat)

BANANAS FOSTER SAUCE (OPTIONAL)

½ cup (112 g) butter or coconut oil

½ cup (100 g) granulated sugar

¼ tsp salt

1 tbsp (15 ml) vanilla extract

2 large bananas, cut into coins

Big splash of rum

To make the filling, in a medium saucepan, add the cashews and cover with water. Bring to a boil and cook for 15 to 20 minutes, or until they are softened. Drain the cashews and add them to a blender with the rest of the filling ingredients and pulse until a pretty smooth paste is made. This may take a few minutes.

To make the batter, in a large mixing bowl or measuring cup, whisk together the milk, eggs, vanilla, rum and granulated sugar. Set aside.

Have an 8 x 8-inch (20 x 20-cm) or 9 x 9-inch (23 x 23-cm) oiled baking dish nearby. Spread ¼ cup (60 g) of the cashew cream between 2 pieces of bread, pressing down to glue them together. Repeat with 6 more slices of bread. Position the sandwiches in the baking dish, cutting them or arranging them so they fit snugly. Pour over half the batter, pressing down on the bread to help it soak up the liquid. Spread the remaining cashew cream evenly over the top of the arranged sandwiches, and then top with the remaining 4 slices of bread to create an even layer. Pour over the rest of the batter, press the bread down again gently, cover it with plastic wrap or foil and let it sit for at least 30 minutes so the bread has a chance to soak up all the liquid.

Preheat the oven to 350°F (180°C or gas mark 4). Remove the foil from the pan, and bake for 30 to 40 minutes, or until the bread is toasted on top and the custard has cooked through. Remove from the oven and serve as is with maple syrup and/or confectioners' sugar or keep in a warm place while you make the Bananas Foster sauce.

To make the sauce, if using, in a small skillet, melt the butter, then stir in the granulated sugar, salt and vanilla. Let it cook until it begins to bubble, then cook for a minute more. Add the bananas in a layer and let them cook for 1 minute, then flip over to cook on the other side for another minute. Shake the pan to mix without breaking the bananas, then remove the pan from the heat and add the rum. It will make a large splash. Return the pan back to the heat, and cook for another 30 seconds or so, shaking the pan until the rum is distributed and the bubbling subsides. Pour over the French toast while still warm.

STRAWBERRY BALSAMIC SHORTCAKE

I'm going to warn you, like any friend would, about the acrid smell of boiling balsamic. There wasn't a wise soul around to keep me from trying to reduce vinegar into a syrup and when I did, the cushions on the living room sofa smelled for days. This is my tangy updo to the sinfully sweet strawberry shortcake.

VEGAN OPTION, WHOLE WHEAT, EGG-FREE
SERVES 6

STRAWBERRIES

2 cups (400 g) hulled and coined strawberries

2 tbsp (24 g) pure cane sugar

OLIVE OIL BISCUITS

3 cups (360 g) whole wheat pastry flour, plus more for dusting

4 tsp (10 g) baking powder

3 tbsp (36 g) granulated sugar

½ tsp salt

½ cup (120 ml) olive oil

½ cup (120 ml) buttermilk, plus more for brushing

Raw sugar, for sprinkling (optional)

BALSAMIC GLAZE

½ cup (120 ml) balsamic vinegar

¼ cup (60 ml) agave or honey

WHIPPED CREAM TOPPING

1 cup (235 ml) cold heavy cream

3 tbsp (45 ml) honey or agave

Mint or basil for topping

To make the strawberries, toss the coined berries and cane sugar together in a bowl. Let them sit for about 20 minutes, or until they start to break down and liquefy.

Preheat the oven to 450°F (230°C or gas mark 8) and have a sheet pan lined with parchment nearby.

To make the biscuits, in a bowl, stir together the flour, baking powder, granulated sugar and salt. Drizzle over the olive oil, and gently toss with your hands until droplets of oil are dispersed evenly throughout the flour. Add the buttermilk, stirring gently and compressing with your hands until a shaggy dough is formed. Dump out onto a floured work surface and knead until it comes together into a solid mass. Roll it out into a 1¼-inch (3-cm)-thick disk. Using a 3-inch (7.5-cm) biscuit cutter, punch out 6 biscuits, folding and re-rolling the dough if needed. Place the biscuits on the lined sheet tray, brush with more buttermilk, sprinkle with raw sugar if using, and bake for 8 to 10 minutes, or until slightly puffed and golden brown. Remove the biscuits and transfer to a wire rack to cool.

To make the balsamic glaze, combine the balsamic vinegar and honey in a saucepan and bring it to a simmer. Cook over medium-low heat for 10 to 15 minutes, or until the liquid reduces by half. Set aside to cool and thicken.

To make the whipped cream topping, when you're ready to serve, beat together the cream and honey in a stand mixer with a whisk attachment, or in a bowl with an electric mixer, until stiff peaks form, about 3 minutes. Split the cooled biscuits in half and spoon on some of the strawberries along with some of their juices so it soaks into the bottom biscuit. Top with a dollop of whipped cream, followed by a drizzle of the balsamic glaze. Top with the other half of the biscuit, and repeat with more strawberries, more cream, and another drizzle of glaze. Repeat with the rest of the biscuits, and serve immediately.

ALTERNATIVE DAIRY: Replace the buttermilk with ½ cup (120 ml) of plant-based milk and 1 tablespoon (15 ml) of lemon juice. Let sit for 5 minutes to curdle and then proceed with the recipe. Replace the whipped cream with cold canned coconut cream whipped with agave or honey to taste and 3 tablespoons (45 ml) of virgin coconut oil.

MAPLE CINNAMON GRANOLA

The perfect granola has always eluded me. It's a recipe I make in a rush, bake at the overzealous oven temperature of 450°F, and forget about halfway through. My miserable oven spits a bit of smoke through its corners, the maple bubbles into black tar and the apartment smells like burnt chalk. It's a smell that screams, "Again?" and "That was Vermont maple, you fool!" I've learned to turn the heat down, something closer to 325°F, and let it slow bake. I'll occasionally set a timer, but it's okay if I forget to do that, too.

VEGAN, GLUTEN-FREE
MAKES 4 CUPS (490 G)

3 cups (240 g) old-fashioned rolled oats

½ cup (120 ml) maple syrup

⅓ cup (80 ml) melted virgin coconut oil or olive oil

2 tsp (5 g) ground cinnamon

2 tsp (10 ml) vanilla extract

¾ tsp coarse sea salt

½ cup (70 g) raw nuts and/or seeds (optional)

⅓ cup (50 g) dried fruit (optional)

Preheat the oven to 325°F (170°C or gas mark 3). Line a baking sheet with parchment paper.

Toss all the ingredients together on the prepared baking sheet, massaging the oats to make sure they're completely coated, and bake for 1 hour, tossing halfway through. If you want clustered granola, be sure to press the mixture into the baking pan with the back of a large spoon before you put it in the oven to bake, and don't agitate it much while baking (a rule that's especially easy for me).

Remove the granola from the oven and allow it to cool completely. Transfer to an airtight container and store in the cabinet for up to 2 months.

OPTIONAL ADD-INS: Hemp seeds, quinoa, any dried fruit (apricots, dates, coconut, mango, strawberries, etc.), any nuts or seeds (sunflower seeds, pumpkin seeds, almonds, pecans, walnuts, etc.), chocolate chips (added after the granola has cooled).

MACADAMIA BROWN BUTTER CASHEW COOKIE DOUGH

For the holidays, I've made it an unfailing tradition to bake my big brother a batch of macadamia nut cookies served with an extra side of cookie dough. First, I toast the nuts lightly on a sheet pan to bring out the oils, because there's nothing like the smell it makes as it browns. That coupled with the nutty scent of the browned butter creates a rich caramel smell that I've started to associate with him being back home. You can barely taste the cashews here, but it's a nice trick to make the no-bake cookie dough creamy and scoopable.

EGG-FREE, GLUTEN-FREE, VEGAN OPTION
MAKES 3 CUPS (750 G)

1 cup (120 g) raw macadamia nuts

½ cup (112 g) butter, dairy-free if desired

2 cups (300 g) cashews, soaked or boiled to soften

½ cup (110 g) packed brown sugar or coconut sugar

2 tsp (10 ml) vanilla extract

1 tsp salt

1½ cups (180 g) oat flour

½ cup (87 g) white chocolate chips (optional)

Gluten-free ice cream cones, for serving (optional)

Preheat the oven to 350°F (180°C or gas mark 4).

Spread the macadamia nuts on a half sheet pan. Bake the nuts for 8 to 10 minutes, or until you begin to smell them and their color turns golden brown. Remove from the oven and allow to cool.

In a saucepan, melt the butter over medium heat. Cook, swirling the pan often, for 5 to 6 minutes, or until it starts to turn golden brown. Once it reaches a certain temperature it will darken quickly, so be sure to watch it—you don't want it to burn. The boiling butter will sound like a water faucet running, and it'll smell rich like caramel. Remove it from the heat and pour the butter into a separate dish to cool completely, leaving behind any burnt bits at the bottom of the pan.

Drain the soaked cashews, add them to a food processor or blender along with the cooled brown butter and pulse until a smooth paste is formed (this may take a few minutes).

Add the cashew butter paste to a large mixing bowl or stand mixer along with the brown sugar, vanilla and salt, and beat until combined. Add the flour and continue to mix until incorporated. Fold in the toasted macadamia nuts and the white chocolate chips, if using. Transfer the mixture to a container and refrigerate until chilled and ready to serve. Scoop into ice cream cones, if you like, and top with any of your other favorite toppings.

OPTIONAL ADD-INS: Toasted pecans, toasted walnuts, toasted sliced almonds, chocolate chips, sprinkles, 1 cup (80 g) of rolled oats, 2 tablespoons (16 g) of peanut butter powder, ¼ cup (30 g) of sifted cocoa powder, shredded coconut.

NOTE: This dough can also be frozen, just allow it to sit on the counter for a few minutes to soften before scooping.

ROSEMARY PITA CHIPS WITH CRISPY BLACK-EYED PEA HUMMUS

Rosemary gently frying in a pan with a bit of smashed garlic brings me back home to holiday mornings when I wake up the family to the smell of cooking breakfast: cubed sweet potatoes crisping in a black skillet alongside piney sprigs of fresh rosemary, garlic and olive oil. I finish the hash with a generous sprinkle of chili powder, and serve it next to a hunk of maple-soaked brioche. That's how the smell of our Christmas usually begins these days.

VEGAN, WHOLE WHEAT
MAKES 4–5 CUPS (400–500 G) CRACKERS OR 2 FLATBREADS

CRISPY BLACK-EYED PEA HUMMUS

1 (14-oz [392-g]) can black-eyed peas, rinsed and drained

¼ cup (60 ml) olive oil, plus more for drizzling

Salt, to taste

1 head garlic

¼ cup (60 g) tahini

¼ cup (60 ml) lemon juice

2 tbsp (30 ml) water

1 tsp ground cumin

ROSEMARY OIL

3–4 cloves garlic

⅓ cup (80 g) olive oil

3 sprigs rosemary

Preheat the oven to 400°F (200°C or gas mark 6), and have a sheet pan lined with parchment nearby.

To make the hummus, spread a few tablespoons (45 g) of the rinsed black-eyed peas on the prepared baking sheet, drizzle with olive oil and sprinkle with salt. Chop the top off the garlic head to reveal the cloves, sprinkle it with olive oil and salt and wrap it in aluminum foil. Place it on the baking sheet with the black-eyed peas, and roast in the oven for 25 to 30 minutes, or until the peas are crispy.

Remove the pan from the oven, unwrap the garlic and squeeze the cloves out into a food processor, discarding the skins. To the garlic, add the rest of the canned black-eyed peas, reserving the roasted ones for the top, the ¼ cup (60 ml) of olive oil, tahini paste, lemon juice, water, cumin and salt to taste. Puree until smooth. Transfer to a serving bowl, and top with the crispy black-eyed peas. Set aside while you make the pita chips.

To make the rosemary oil, smash the garlic with the side of your knife and a heavy fist to remove the skins and release the oils. Add them to a small saucepan, along with the olive oil and rosemary, being sure to completely submerge everything in the oil. Bring the oil to a gentle boil for 1 minute, turn off the heat and let the oil steep for 15 to 30 minutes. It'll continue to boil slightly and perfume as it sits.

(continued)

ROSEMARY PITA CHIPS WITH CRISPY BLACK-EYED PEA HUMMUS (CONT.)

To make the pita chips, place the sweet potatoes in a covered pot filled with water, bring to a boil, reduce the heat and boil until tender, 10 to 15 minutes. Drain the potatoes, and blend them in a blender or food processor with the salt, infused rosemary olive oil, cooked garlic and some of the rosemary leaves (discard the stems). Blend until smooth.

Transfer the mixture to a mixing bowl, add the flour and knead until the dough comes together into a smooth ball, about 5 minutes. Divide the dough in half, shape them into balls and let them rest for 15 to 20 minutes under a damp towel to relax the gluten.

Preheat the oven to 400°F (200°C or gas mark 6), and have an oiled baking sheet nearby.

Using a rolling pin, roll out one of the dough balls on a lightly floured surface until it's about ⅛-inch (3-mm) thick. Cut the dough into triangles or preferred shapes, transfer the cut pieces to the oiled baking sheet, drizzle the tops with more oil, sprinkle them with sea salt and chili powder, if using, and bake for 20 to 25 minutes, or until crispy, tossing occasionally. Remove from the oven, and serve warm with the black-eyed pea hummus.

NOTE: Store the crackers in an airtight zip-top bag for up to 2 weeks on the counter.

TIP: This recipe is also easily a flatbread recipe. Simply knead the dough for 3 minutes, let it rest for 10 minutes, then proceed with rolling it out.

PITA CHIPS

4 small sweet potatoes (¾ pound [340 g]), peeled and cut into bite-size chunks

2–2½ cups (240–300 g) white whole wheat flour, plus more for dusting

Olive oil, for drizzling

1 tsp sea salt, plus more for sprinkling

Chili powder, for sprinkling (optional)

APPLE CIDER MONKEY BREAD

There's a doughnut shop tucked away in the corner of the Boston Public Market not too far from Faneuil Hall. One day, I walked into the large building exhausted from a stroll through the rambunctious produce stalls at Haymarket, and might've passed by the small countertop had it not been for the glorious, wafting incense of buttery cinnamon and cider seeping toward my walking path. These people's apple cider doughnut holes can and will steal a crowd just by turning on a ceiling fan. And I'm sure anyone living on our apartment floor will say the same about this monkey bread. I love knowing I can grab people's attention so subtly. This recipe brings me back to my first-ever monkey bread Christmas morning.

EGG-FREE, VEGAN OPTION
MAKES 1 LOAF

DOUGH

3 tbsp (45 g) packed brown sugar

¼ cup (60 ml) warm water, at 115°F (46ºC)

2 tsp (6 g) active dry yeast

3–3½ cups (360–420 g) white whole wheat flour, divided

½ tsp salt

¾ cup (180 ml) warm milk

3 tbsp (45 ml) apple cider vinegar

½ cup (112 g) softened butter

APPLE CIDER COATING

¾ cup (150 g) packed brown sugar

2 tsp (3 g) ground cinnamon

¼ cup (60 g) applesauce

2 tbsp (30 ml) apple cider vinegar

1 tsp salt

4 tbsp (56 g) softened butter

To make the dough, add the brown sugar to the bowl of warm water. Sprinkle the yeast over the top, and let it bloom until a cap of foam forms on the top, 5 to 10 minutes.

In a stand mixer with a dough hook attachment, combine 2½ cups (300 g) of the flour and the salt. Mix on low speed, pouring in the warm milk, apple cider vinegar and bloomed yeast mixture. Add about ½ cup (60 g) more of flour and knead until all the flour is mixed in, then add the butter and mix until the butter is completely worked in. Add extra flour gradually just until the dough comes off the sides of the bowl. You may not need all the flour. Take the dough out of the bowl and place it in a clean, oiled bowl. Cover with plastic wrap or a damp clean kitchen towel and allow to rise in a warm, dark place for 1 to 1½ hours, or until doubled in size.

To make the coating, whisk together the brown sugar, cinnamon, applesauce, apple cider vinegar, salt and butter in a bowl. Oil a Bundt pan and drizzle 3 to 4 tablespoons (45 to 60 ml) of the coating on the bottom of the pan.

Once the dough has risen, punch it down in the center to release the air. Pinch off about 1½-inch (3.8-cm) balls from the dough, roll it into a ball and submerge it in the coating. Place the drenched ball into the Bundt pan. Continue until all the balls are coated and arranged in the pan. If there is any leftover coating, drizzle it over the top of the dough. Cover the pan with plastic wrap and let the dough rise for another 30 to 40 minutes, or until doubled in size.

(continued)

APPLE CIDER MONKEY BREAD (CONT.)

To make the glaze, melt the butter, applesauce, brown sugar and salt together in a saucepan on the stove top or in a bowl in the microwave. Set aside.

Preheat the oven to 350°F (180°C or gas mark 4) and position a rack in the center of the oven.

Remove the plastic from the risen monkey bread, and bake for 25 to 30 minutes, or until cooked through, and it passes the toothpick/skewer test. Remove the monkey bread from the oven and carefully flip it out onto a serving tray while hot. Drizzle it with the apple glaze, and serve warm.

NOTE: The bread can be assembled the day before and left in the fridge to slow rise overnight. The next day, remove the loaf from the fridge and allow it to come to room temperature for at least 30 minutes before baking.

VEGAN OPTION: Replace the butter with virgin coconut oil, at room temperature, or dairy-free butter, and make sure the milk is plant-based.

APPLE GLAZE

2 tbsp (28 g) butter

2 tbsp (30 g) applesauce

5 tbsp (62 g) packed brown sugar

Pinch of salt

PLUM CHAI PIE

I love steeping bags of chai tea in boiling water and bringing out the floral bits from the cardamom, clove and the heat from the ginger. Those aromas paired with ripe summer plums make my kitchen smell like potpourri.

WHOLE WHEAT, EGG-FREE, VEGAN OPTION
MAKES ONE 9-INCH (23-CM) PIE

CRUST

2¼ cups (270 g) whole wheat pastry flour

1 tsp salt

1 cup (225 g) cold butter, cut into cubes, or very cold virgin coconut oil

1 tbsp (15 ml) white vinegar

½ cup (120 ml) ice cold water, plus more if needed

CHAI SPICE

2 sticks cinnamon

20 cardamom pods

10 whole cloves

1 tsp fennel seeds

½ tsp salt

½ tsp black peppercorns

FILLING

5–6 plums, pitted and sliced

1-inch (2.5-cm) thumb fresh ginger, peeled and grated

½ cup (100 g) pure cane sugar

Juice of 1 lemon and zest of ½ lemon

¼ cup (30 g) flour

Nut or grain milk or cream, for brushing

Raw sugar, for sprinkling (optional)

To make the crust, combine the flour and salt in a large bowl, and then toss in the cubes of butter. Cut the butter into the flour using your hands or a pastry cutter until the flour is a little crumbly, but there are still pieces of butter the size of flattened chickpeas. Add the vinegar and the cold water, 2 tablespoons (30 ml) at a time, stirring gently and compressing with your hands just until the dough comes together. Divide the dough in half, shape the halves into disks, wrap them in plastic wrap and refrigerate for at least 20 minutes.

To make the chai spice, grind all the spices in a food processor until fine like a powder.

To make the filling, combine sliced plums, grated ginger, sugar, lemon juice, lemon zest, flour and the chai spice blend. Toss everything together to coat and let it sit and marinate for a few minutes.

Preheat the oven to 400°F (200°C or gas mark 6) and have a 9-inch (23-cm) pie plate nearby.

Remove one of the chilled disks of dough from the fridge. Using a lightly dusted rolling pin, roll it out into a ¼-inch (6-mm)-thick round on a lightly floured surface. Fold the dough over the rolling pin to help ease it into the pie dish, making sure to fill out all the corners of the dish. Leave a 1-inch (2.5-cm) overhang, and trim off any excess. Fill the pan with the plums and all their juices.

Remove the other disk of dough from the fridge, roll it out into a ¼-inch (6-mm)-thick round and drape it on top of the fruit, also trimming off all but a 1-inch (2.5-cm) overhang from the dough. Pinch the edges of the crusts together to seal. Cut a few slits in the middle of the top crust so steam can release when it bakes. Place the pie in the freezer for another 10 minutes to chill the butter in the crust.

Remove the pie from the freezer, and brush the top of the crust with milk. Sprinkle with the raw sugar, if using, and bake for 35 to 40 minutes, or until the top is golden brown and the filling is bubbling. Remove from the oven and allow to cool for at least 20 minutes before slicing and serving.

PAPAYA PASTRIES

I grew up around papaya, its funky smell tyrannizing all the other fruit in my fruit salad. I used to turn my nose up to it, pick it out and toss it onto another tray. I've learned since then that cooking it down to turn it into a fruit juice or puree helps soften the odor. These pastries are inspired by the times I travel back home to Florida and we drive down to Calle Ocho, eat a family dinner at Little Havana and order a dozen pastelitos—guava and cream pastries—with a side of powerful Cuban coffee.

EGG-FREE, VEGAN OPTION
MAKES 8 PASTRIES

2½ lb ripe whole papaya or 2 lb (900 g) peeled and chunked papaya

½ cup (100 g) pure cane sugar

1 tsp salt

2 tbsp (16 g) tapioca flour

8 sheets whole wheat phyllo dough, defrosted

½ cup (112 g) unsalted butter, melted, or ½ cup (120 ml) neutral oil

1 (8-oz [224-g]) package cream cheese, cut into 8 (1-oz [28-g]) strips (dairy-free if desired)

To make the papaya paste, peel the papaya, discard the black seeds and chop the flesh into chunks. Add the chunks to a food processor or blender and puree until completely smooth. You may need to do this in batches depending on the size of your blender. Add the pureed papaya to a medium saucepan, along with the sugar and salt. Cook over medium heat, stirring occasionally so it doesn't burn, until the liquid is reduced to one-fourth of the volume, about 45 minutes. Place a tilted lid on the pot so the mixture doesn't splatter onto the stove top. After the papaya has reduced, add the tapioca flour and cook, whisking constantly, until it thickens, about 3 minutes. Transfer the mixture to a small container and chill in the fridge for 2 hours or until solid enough to cut.

Preheat the oven to 400°F (200°C or gas mark 6) and have a lined sheet pan nearby.

Remove the papaya paste from the fridge and cut into eight 1½-ounce (42-g) strips. Set aside.

Unwrap the defrosted phyllo dough and lay it out on the countertop. Cover the dough with a sheet of plastic wrap and place a damp cloth on top to make sure they don't dry out while you work.

Lay a sheet of phyllo out on a work surface. Brush the top lightly with some of the melted butter, then fold the sheet in half widthwise. Rotate the sheet so the shorter end is facing you, then brush the surface again with more butter, fold it in half widthwise and brush the top with more butter. On the bottom corner triangle of the sheet, stack a strip of cream cheese and a strip of papaya paste. Fold the triangle up over itself, and keep folding it up until the triangle is wrapped. Place it seam-side down on the sheet pan, and brush the top with more melted butter. Repeat for the other 7 pastries, and then bake in the oven for 12 to 15 minutes, or until golden brown and crispy. Serve warm or at room temperature.

NOTE: The pastries can stay on the countertop, sealed in an airtight container, for up to 2 days, or kept in the fridge for up to 1 week. Toast in the oven to reheat.

CAKE DOUGHNUTS WITH COFFEE GLAZE

To me, every doughnut shop smells the same. I walk in and inhale the microscopic particles of confectioners' sugar floating everywhere. I smell the grease droplets from the stale frying oil, and finally, the brewed coffee, all too often sweetened with the strong lacquer of hazelnut syrup. Those three smells, and I'm brought back to weekend mornings when my mother would surprise us with a trip over to the cubbyhole of a doughnut shop in our strip mall down the street. I'd stand at the foot of the counter and point up to the cake doughnuts with the icing glaze. And nothing has changed. I'm still that same girl.

30 MINUTES OR LESS, VEGAN, WHOLE WHEAT
MAKES 12 DOUGHNUTS

CAKE DOUGHNUTS

½ cup (120 ml) milk (grain or nut)

2 tbsp (30 g) yogurt (coconut or other plant-based yogurt)

½ cup (112 g) unsalted butter, softened, or virgin coconut oil

¾ cup (150 g) granulated sugar

1 tbsp (15 ml) vanilla extract

⅓ cup (80 g) applesauce, at room temperature

2 cups (240 g) whole wheat pastry flour

1 tbsp (8 g) baking powder

½ tsp salt

¼ cup (50 g) rainbow sprinkles

COFFEE GLAZE

½ cup (120 ml) hot brewed coffee

½ cup (60 g) confectioners' sugar, sifted

½ tsp vanilla extract

¼ tsp hazelnut extract (optional)

Preheat the oven to 350°F (180°C or gas mark 4) and have 2 oiled 6-cavity doughnut pans nearby.

To make the doughnuts, in a small bowl, combine the milk and yogurt, and set aside.

In a large bowl with a handheld electric beater, cream the butter, granulated sugar and vanilla until fluffy, about 3 minutes. Slowly drizzle in the applesauce and continue to beat until incorporated.

In a separate bowl, sift the flour, baking powder and salt together, then mix in the rainbow sprinkles. Add the dry ingredients to the creamed butter and sugar mixture in three batches, alternating with the milk and yogurt mixture, and folding gently until everything is just combined. Fill the donut pans three-fourths of the way full, and bake them until you can insert a toothpick into the center and it comes out clean, 8 to 12 minutes. Remove them from the oven and transfer to a wire rack to cool slightly while you mix the glaze.

To make the coffee glaze, whisk all the ingredients together in a mixing bowl. Dip the tops of the doughnuts into the glaze and transfer them to a wire rack, glaze-side up. Serve.

ONION AND RED PEPPER QUICHE

Sweet onions slow-browning in a pot of olive oil is probably my favorite smell. Anytime my mom would start cooking anything, she always started with her speckled blue, deep-dish pot, a puddle of oil and diced yellow onions. Now that I live in Fenway, 10 feet away from the baseball park, I'm overcome with feelings of being back home when I smell the onions and peppers wafting through my screened window and watch the crowds of people gather, lining up in front of the sausage stands.

MAKES ONE 4 X 14-INCH (10 X 36-CM) TART

CRUST

1½ cups (180 g) whole wheat pastry flour

½ tsp salt

½ cup (112 g) plus 5 tbsp (70 g) cold unsalted butter, cut into cubes

6–7 tbsp (90–105 ml) ice cold water, divided

FILLING

3 medium yellow onions, thinly sliced

3 tbsp (45 ml) olive oil

1 large red bell pepper, cored, ribs removed and cut long thin strips

½ tsp red pepper flakes

1 tsp salt, divided

3 large eggs

⅓ cup (80 ml) milk

½ cup (112 g) plain nonfat Greek yogurt

2 tsp (8 g) country-style mustard

NOTE: Replace the crust with thawed store-bought puff pastry, if you like.

To make the crust, combine the flour and salt in a mixing bowl. Cut the cubed butter into the flour with the back of a fork or with your hands until the flour is crumbly with chunks of butter still visible. Add 4 to 5 tablespoons (60 to 75 ml) of the water, tossing and compressing the dough slightly. Then add the remaining water, 1 tablespoon (15 ml) at a time, until the crust just comes together into a shaggy ball. You may not need all the water. The dough shouldn't be dry but it shouldn't be tacky either. Shape the dough into a rough 3 x 6-inch (7.5 x 15-cm) rectangle, wrap in plastic wrap and refrigerate for 20 to 30 minutes.

To make the filling, in a large deep-dish skillet or saucepan, toss together the thinly sliced onions and olive oil, then turn the heat on to medium and cook until translucent, 8 or so minutes, tossing occasionally, making sure the onions never brown. Add the sliced red bell pepper, red pepper flakes and ½ teaspoon of the salt and continue to cook for another 10 to 15 minutes, stirring occasionally, until the peppers have completely softened and the mixture has compacted. Set aside to cool.

Remove the dough from the fridge and using a lightly dusted rolling pin on a lightly dusted surface, roll it out into a 6 x 24-inch (15 x 61-cm) rectangle, then starting from the short end, fold the dough in thirds. Roll it out to the same size, then fold it in thirds again. Roll it out to half the size, fold it in half, then turn the dough and fold it in thirds so it's compacted. Place it in the fridge for another 20 minutes.

In a bowl, whisk together the eggs, milk, yogurt, mustard and remaining ½ teaspoon salt and set aside.

Preheat the oven to 350°F (180°C or gas mark 4) and have a 4 x 14-inch (10 x 36-cm) tart pan nearby. Remove the dough from the fridge, roll it out a little larger than the size of the tart pan and gently transfer it to the tart pan, easing it into the edges and corners. Trim away all but a 1-inch (2.5-cm) border around the edges of the crust, and fold the edges up to create a taller border. Spread the cooked onions and peppers across the dough and pour over the whisked egg mixture. Bake for 25 to 30 minutes, or until the eggs are puffed and the edges of the crust are golden brown. Remove from the oven and allow to cool for 10 minutes before cutting. Serve warm or at room temperature.

BANANA S'MORES PIZZA

I taught myself to roast marshmallows on an electric stove, so my first encounter with their smell was absent of burning wood and smoke. I'd huddle over a full bag of marshmallows, pierce through a spongy square with my skewer and hold it inches away from the hot coil, turning it, watching it closely and pulling back before it could melt onto the burner. I love that smell, but I'd pass on all that work. I'd rather broil an entire bag at once.

30 MINUTES OR LESS, EGG-FREE, GLUTEN-FREE
MAKES ONE 20-INCH (50-CM) PIZZA

MASCARPONE TOPPING

½ vanilla bean or 2 tsp (10 ml) vanilla extract

½ cup (113 g) mascarpone cheese

2 tbsp (28 g) softened butter or coconut oil

1 cup (175 g) semisweet chocolate chips

6 oz (168 g) natural mini marshmallows or regular, quartered

¼ cup (35 g) chopped hazelnuts (optional)

BANANA PIZZA CRUST

2 large bananas

½ cup (64 g) coconut flour

¼ tsp salt

2 tbsp (28 g) softened butter or coconut oil

Preheat the oven to 425°F (220°C or gas mark 7) and have a lined sheet pan ready.

To make the topping, slice the vanilla bean in half lengthwise, and then using the back of a knife, press and scrape the seeds out of the bean. Add the seeds to a small bowl along with the mascarpone cheese and softened butter.

To make the crust, blend the bananas in a food processor or blender until smooth. Add the coconut flour, salt and softened butter, and pulse until it comes together into a ball of dough.

Dump the dough out onto a sheet of parchment paper, place another sheet of parchment paper on top and roll it out evenly into a 20-inch (50-cm) round. Transfer the crust to a baking sheet, removing the top sheet of parchment paper and bake for 12 to 15 minutes, or until the crust bubbles and browns. Remove from the oven, pressing down any air pockets in the dough, and turn the oven heat to broil and position an oven rack at the highest position.

To the hot crust, sprinkle on the chocolate chips. To help the chocolate melt, cover the pan loosely with foil and leave for 1 minute. Remove the foil and smooth the melted chocolate evenly over the dough. Place dollops of the mascarpone mixture over the chocolate, scatter the marshmallows and hazelnuts, if using, on top and broil for 1 to 3 minutes, or until the marshmallows char—watch it carefully. Remove from the oven, slice and serve.

ALTERNATIVE FLOURS: You can use almond flour, almond meal flour or other nut flours.

SMOKED BBQ ROASTED VEGGIES

If there's a family reunion and fried fish and spaghetti isn't getting served, then there's barbecue instead, with pools of thick smoke that drift from the cracks of black cylindrical grills bolted to the park grounds, latching onto me, lingering in my clothes days later. And like the smell that stayed in the fabric of my favorite summer peplum dresses, they lasted in my memory, too, along with memories of sticky fingers, soiled napkins, loud music and even louder laughter. When it came to big family gatherings, this is what we are about.

Vegan, gluten-free
Serves 8–12

BBQ Sauce

2–3 tbsp (30–45 ml) olive oil

½ red onion, chopped

3 cloves garlic, minced

¼ tsp crushed red pepper flakes

½ cup (120 ml) apple cider vinegar

¼ cup (55 g) packed brown sugar

¼ cup (60 g) tomato paste

3 tbsp (33 g) country-style Dijon mustard

¼ cup (60 ml) water, plus more for thinning

Salt, to taste

Roasted Veggies

3 lb (1.4 kg) fresh vegetables, washed and trimmed of stems and brown bits (I used green beans, tomatoes, carrots, sweet potatoes, heads of garlic and zucchini)

Olive oil, for drizzling

¾ cup (110 g) smoked almonds, roughly chopped

To make the sauce, in a medium saucepan over medium high heat, heat the olive oil, then add the red onion and cook, stirring occasionally, until tender, 5 to 6 minutes. Add the garlic and red pepper flakes and cook until fragrant, another minute. Deglaze the pan with the apple cider vinegar, stirring to scrape up any brown bits from the pan, and add the brown sugar, tomato paste, Dijon mustard, water and salt to taste. Bring the sauce to a boil, then reduce the heat to a simmer. Cook for another 5 minutes, then remove from the heat. Add more water if the sauce is too thick for your liking.

Preheat the oven to 425°F (220°C or gas mark 7) and have a half sheet pan nearby.

Cut the vegetables into long spears or chunks that are relatively the same size, spread them out on the baking sheet, drizzle them with olive oil and then pour over the BBQ sauce. Toss everything to coat, and then roast for 25 to 30 minutes, or until crispy and tender but not soft and mushy. Remove from the oven, sprinkle over the smoked almonds and serve.

SOUND: SNAP, CRUNCH AND MUSIC

Sometimes I forget how powerful sounds can be in connection with the foods I cook or eat until I make it a point to listen, I can tell the quality of a good chocolate bar by the pitch of its snap, or how crispy croutons are by the way they chafe against the sheet tray—same goes for nuts and seeds. Then there's the absence of sound, which is equally as helpful; I know my oven-baked rice is done when the kernels stop popping against the underbelly of the aluminum foil. I also know to eat faster when my bowl of cereal slows its crackling—unless, of course, I happen to be in the mood for a soggy, milk-bloated breakfast. I have memories, too, of R&B and hip hop music changing my expectations of food by just being present and connected to big food moments. It's funny how this simple sense can impact the final flavor.

POP BISCUITS

Some Sunday mornings we'd accidentally leave frozen cans of biscuit dough defrosting on the counter for too long, and when the growing yeast couldn't stay contained inside the tube anymore, suddenly we'd hear this loud "POP" from the kitchen that'd scream to us it was time to bake them already.

MAKES 6–8 BISCUITS
VEGAN OPTION

½ cup (120 ml) water, warmed to 120°F (49°C)

2 tbsp (25 g) sugar

1 (2½-tsp [9-g]) packet active dry yeast

1¾ cups (210 g) unbleached all-purpose flour, plus more for dusting

½ tsp salt

6 tbsp (85 g) cold butter, dairy-free if you like

Add the water to a bowl with the sugar. Sprinkle over the yeast and let it sit until a cap of froth forms on the top, 5 to 10 minutes. Add the bloomed yeast to a large mixing bowl along with the flour and salt, and knead all the ingredients together for 1 to 2 minutes, just until smooth. Add a little more flour if the dough is unbearable sticky, but not too much to make the dough stiff. Place the dough in a clean, oiled bowl, cover it with plastic wrap and let it rest for 60 minutes.

Once the dough has rested, lightly flour your work surface and a rolling pin and roll it into a rectangle with a height 3 times its width. The dough should not be too warm.

Using the rolling pin, bang the cold butter until it becomes just malleable enough to flatten into a rough rectangular shape. Place the flattened butter across the middle third of the dough, then fold the edges of the dough over the butter to encase it completely. There should be no creases or holes for the butter to escape. Fold the dough over itself 5 or 6 times, rolling it back out to the original size after each fold and dusting the dough lightly if it ever starts to stick to your work surface. Let the dough rest if it gets too tough and hard to stretch and roll.

Using a 2-inch (5-cm) cookie cutter, cut out 6 biscuits and place on a baking sheet lined with parchment. Repeat with the other piece of dough and the second stick of butter. If you need to roll the dough out a second time, that's fine. Cover the biscuits loosely with plastic wrap and place in a warm place to double in size, about an hour, or in the fridge to slow rise overnight.

When you're ready to bake the biscuits, preheat the oven to 425°F (220°C or gas mark 7). If you kept the biscuits in the fridge overnight, let them to come to room temperature first. Then, remove the plastic wrap and bake them for 12 to 15 minutes, or until puffed and golden brown on top. Serve warm with jam, if you like.

BANANA PUDDING CROUTON PARFAITS

I love making croutons: tearing old bread into jagged chunks, tossing them around on a cookie sheet with oily hands, then throwing them under the broiler to get even crunchier. The idea of starting with something pillow soft, like bread or cake, drying it out and then saturating and softening it again with liquid reminds me a lot of the life span of a vanilla wafer in banana pudding.

EGG-FREE, GLUTEN-FREE, VEGAN OPTION
MAKES 2 PARFAITS

BANANA CAKE CROUTONS

⅓ cup (80 g) semisolid virgin coconut oil or softened butter

2 tbsp (30 ml) maple syrup

1 tbsp (15 ml) vanilla extract

2 ripe bananas, pureed in a blender

2 cups (240 g) oat flour

2 tsp (6 g) baking powder

½ tsp salt

⅓ cup (80 ml) oat or nut milk

PARFAITS

5 ripe bananas, 3 mashed, 2 sliced

3 cups (720 g) plain nonfat Greek yogurt or plant-based yogurt, divided

1 tsp vanilla extract

1–2 tbsp (15–30 ml) agave, to taste

Preheat the oven to 350°F (180°C or gas mark 4) and have an oiled rimmed 9 x 13-inch (23 x 33-cm) sheet tray nearby.

To make the cake croutons, in a large mixing bowl, cream together the softened coconut oil, maple syrup and vanilla until fluffy. Gradually add the pureed banana, mixing until combined. Sift the flour, baking powder and salt into the bowl, folding gently, then add the milk and finish folding until just combined. Pour the batter into the sheet tray, spreading evenly to the edges of the pan, and bake for 15 to 20 minutes, or until the cake is cooked all the way through. Remove the cake from the oven and allow to cool completely. Reduce the oven temperature to 325°F (170°C or gas mark 3).

Cut the cake into bite-size pieces, then place the cubes back on the sheet tray and bake for another 35 to 40 minutes, tossing the croutons halfway through. Remove from the oven and allow to cool and harden.

When you're ready to assemble the parfaits, have 2 glasses on hand. In a bowl, mix 2 of the mashed bananas with 2 cups (480 g) of the Greek yogurt, vanilla and agave to taste. Set aside. Add the last mashed banana to a bowl and set aside. Add the remaining 1 cup (240 g) of yogurt to a disposable piping bag with a star tip. Spoon some of the yogurt and banana mixture into the bottom of the glasses. Top with some of the banana croutons, followed by some of the mashed bananas, some of the sliced bananas and a piping of the plain yogurt. Repeat the layering until the glasses are filled. I like to end with a decorative piping of the yogurt, and then garnish with crumbled croutons and a couple of banana slices on top. Serve immediately, or cover with plastic wrap and keep in the fridge for up to 2 days. The cake will soften as it sits.

NOTE: If you plan to make the parfait in advance, hold off on garnishing with the sliced banana, because they will brown.

TIP: When making the croutons, if you're starting with frozen bananas, let them come to room temperature completely before adding them to the creamed fat and sugar; otherwise, it will seize up.

BRÛLÉED BUTTER-MILK PIE

My great-aunt Doris recently shared her buttermilk pie recipe with me over the phone. I swore something got lost in translation when a cup of melted margarine pooled to the top, burning the sugar and eggs in the pie. It reminded me of crème brûlée. I remembered cracking the surface of my very first pot of crème brûlée. A gentle whack from my spoon's edge, and the sugar split like an eggshell, revealing underneath it the smoothest custard I'd ever eaten. Now, great anticipation builds in me right before splitting hard sugar, right before I hear that subtle "tkkK . . ." And I knew I needed to add that sound to this recipe.

EGG-FREE, VEGAN OPTION
MAKES ONE 9-INCH (23-CM) PIE

CRUST

1 cup (120 g) whole wheat pastry flour, plus more for dusting

½ tsp salt

6 tbsp (84 g) cold butter, cut into ½" (1.3-cm) cubes

3 tbsp (45 ml) cold buttermilk

FILLING

1½ cups (355 ml) buttermilk

⅓ cup (75 g) pure cane sugar

2 tsp (10 ml) vanilla extract

¼ tsp salt

¼ cup (30 g) flour

TOP LAYER

6 tbsp (72 g) pure cane sugar

Fresh berries, for serving (optional)

VEGAN OPTION: Replace the butter with dairy-free butter. See page 200 for vegan buttermilk.

To make the crust, in a mixing bowl, stir together the flour and salt, then toss in the cubes of cold butter to coat. Using your thumb and index finger, squish the pieces of butter to flatten, and continue to break the butter up until 50 percent of the butter is crumbly, but not completely uniform in texture; you want there to be chickpea-size nuggets of butter still present. Add the cold buttermilk 1 tablespoon (15 ml) at a time, blending and gathering the mixture with your hands until a dough is formed. Shape the dough into a disk, wrap in plastic wrap and refrigerate for at least 30 minutes. While the dough is chilling, prepare the filling.

To make the filling, add the buttermilk, sugar, vanilla, salt and flour to a blender or food processor and blend until smooth. Let the filling rest while the dough chills. Have ready a 9-inch (23-cm) pie dish.

Once the dough is chilled, roll it out on a lightly floured surface or between 2 sheets of parchment paper into a 20-inch (50-cm) round. Wrap the dough around the rolling pin to help ease it into the pie dish, then crimp the edges into a pattern with your fingers or a fork. Place the crust in the freezer to harden for another 10 to 15 minutes.

Preheat the oven to 350°F (180°C or gas mark 4) and position a rack in the center of the oven. Remove the unbaked crust from the freezer and bake for 12 to 15 minutes, or until the pie turns light golden brown. Remove from the oven and pour in the filling mixture. Bake for 25 to 30 minutes, or until the center is set and doesn't jiggle when shaken. Remove from the oven. I like to serve mine warm from the oven, but if you'd prefer it chilled, place it in the fridge for at least 2 hours or until ready to serve.

For the top layer, when it's time to serve, add the sugar to a small saucepan. Cook over medium heat until the sugar begins to brown and bubble. Swirl the pan to help any uncooked sugar liquefy and cook for a few more seconds, then pour it out over the cold buttermilk pie. Working quickly, carefully tilt the pie dish to evenly distribute the browned sugar over the top. Allow to cool and harden for about 5 minutes, and serve immediately by cracking the top and slicing. Top with fresh berries, if desired.

NO-BAKE NUT AND FRUIT BARS

I get a strange satisfaction when I dump and spread nuts and seeds out onto a baking tray and hear their hard shells chafe against the raw metal. Be sure to catch that sound if you can. These bars are nutty, filling and have the perfect amount of natural sweetness.

30 MINUTES OR LESS, VEGAN OPTION, GLUTEN FREE
MAKES 12 BARS

1½ cups (255 g) raw almonds

½ cup (72 g) raw cashews

1 cup (145 g) shelled sunflower seeds or pumpkin seeds

½ cup (60 g) ground flax or chia seeds

½ cup (75 g) dried blueberries or other diced dried fruit

½ cup (120 ml) honey or maple syrup

2 tbsp (30 ml) olive oil

2 tsp (10 ml) vanilla extract

1 tsp salt

Preheat the oven to 375°F (190°C or gas mark 5). Have an 8 x 5-inch (20 x 12.5-cm) baking dish oiled and lined with a strip of parchment nearby.

Spread the almonds, cashews, seeds and flax meal on a sheet pan, and bake in the oven for 10 to 12 minutes, or until the nuts are brown and toasted. Remove from the oven and allow to cool, then transfer to a large mixing bowl along with the dried blueberries.

In a saucepan, bring the honey, olive oil, vanilla and salt to a boil. Cook until it turns a chestnut brown color, 10 to 12 minutes. Remove from the heat and pour over the toasted nuts and seeds, tossing quickly with a wooden spoon to coat. Then quickly dump the mixture into the oiled baking dish, spreading out evenly with the back of a spoon. Allow at least 30 minutes to cool and harden, then cut and serve.

NOTE: Keep the granola bars in an airtight zip-top on the counter or in the freezer for optimal shelf life.

OPTIONAL ADD-INS: Puffed quinoa, freeze-dried strawberries, ground cinnamon, drizzled chocolate on top.

CINNAMON TOAST CRUNCH BARS

This is the story of why I never share my cereal and milk: I was about seven or eight, and a couple of my cousins slept over the house. My dad called us into the den to serve us cereal for breakfast, and when I peered across our huge table that sliced off my body from the neck down, I saw my droopy-eyed cousin, who had a line of dried drool running up the side of his cheek and a line of dried snot under his nose. He stared back at me with dead eyes, then dipped his spoon into the milk, brought it up to his lips, and slurped hard and long. The milk dribbled down his chubby chin, and I lost my appetite, FOREVER! Now eating milk and cereal is a private activity, otherwise I just snack on the cereal dry.

VEGAN
MAKES 8 BARS

CRUNCH BARS

¼ cup (60 ml) maple syrup

½ cup (100 g) coconut sugar or packed brown sugar

¼ cup (60 g) almond butter or cashew butter

⅓ cup (80 ml) neutral oil

1 tsp vanilla extract

½ tsp salt

2 tsp (5 g) ground cinnamon

½ tsp ground allspice

1½ cups (180 g) white whole wheat flour or spelt flour

1 tsp baking powder

ICING

4 tbsp (56 g) virgin coconut oil or butter

1 tbsp (15 g) almond butter or cashew butter

6 tbsp (70 g) sugar

1 tbsp (8 g) ground cinnamon

Preheat the oven to 350°F (180°C or gas mark 4) and have a lined 8 or 9-inch (20 or 23-cm) square baking dish nearby—the size is dependent on whether you want thicker or thinner bars.

To make the bars, in a large bowl, whisk together the maple syrup, sugar, almond butter, oil, vanilla, salt, cinnamon and allspice. Then, using a wooden spoon, stir in the flour and baking powder. The mixture will be thick. Transfer it to the baking dish, and press it down firmly into an even layer. You can use a piece of parchment paper or wax paper to help. Bake the bar for 20 minutes, then lower the oven temperature to 275°F (140°C or gas mark 1), remove the pan, and gently cut the bar into eight 1 x 4-inch (2.5 x 10-cm) bars. Set aside while you make the icing.

To make the icing, in a small saucepan over low heat, combine the coconut oil, almond butter, sugar and cinnamon and cook until the mixture loosens. Transfer the warm icing to a piping bag or squeeze bottle with a small tip, and pipe swirls over the bars. If the mixer starts to seize up, run the bag or bottle under hot water until it loosens again. Place the bars back in the oven to cook for another 20 to 25 minutes. Remove and allow to cool before eating—overnight is best for optimum crispiness.

PEACHES AND CREAM CAKE

I was ten years old when 112, the R&B boy band, released their single "Peaches and Cream." Then I realized that eating a peach was much more than just eating a peach, at that moment it became sensual and taboo. But it's such an amazing pairing. I'm letting myself indulge.

EGG-FREE, WHOLE WHEAT
MAKES ONE 9-INCH (23-CM) CAKE

2 ripe peaches, pitted and sliced

Juice of 1 lemon

2 tsp (5 g) ground cinnamon

2 cups (240 g) white whole wheat flour or all-purpose flour

1 tbsp (8 g) baking powder

½ tsp salt

¾ cup (90 g) sour cream

⅔ cup (160 ml) milk

¾ cup (168 g) butter, softened

1 cup (200 g) sugar

2 tsp (10 ml) vanilla extract

Sweetened whipped cream, for serving (optional)

Toss the sliced peaches together with the lemon juice and cinnamon. Set aside to marinate while you make the cake.

Preheat the oven to 350°F (180°C or gas mark 4) and have an oiled 9-inch (23-cm) springform pan nearby.

In a bowl, sift together the flour, baking powder and salt. In a separate small bowl, stir together the sour cream and milk until smooth.

In a large mixing bowl with an electric handheld beater or in a stand mixer with a paddle attachment, cream the butter, sugar and vanilla until fluffy. Fold in the flour in 2 batches, alternating with the sour cream mixture, and mix until just combined, being careful not to overmix. Pour half the batter into the cake pan, smoothing the top. Layer the peaches and their juices evenly on top, and then add the last of the cake batter, smoothing the top. Bake for 40 to 45 minutes, or until a toothpick inserted into the center comes out clean. Remove from the oven and allow to cool for at least 20 minutes before slicing. Serve with sweetened whipped cream, if you like.

LITTLE CARAMEL CRUNCH BARK

I remember getting dropped off at my aunt's house down in Delray when I was a little girl. She kept a stash of those Little Debbie Star Crunch crisp rice cookies in the closet in her room behind a stack of clothes. As soon as she'd leave for work, I'd break into her room, dig behind her pile of folded jeans, slip a cookie from the box, unwrap it and sink my teeth into the crispy disk . . . I loved hearing the puffed rice crackle beneath the weight of my teeth, and as I'd pull away, I'd see the caramel between the kernels stretch and go white. Now that I'm grown, I'm adding some nut protein and better fats to keep me feeling good while I sneak bites throughout the day.

GLUTEN-FREE, VEGAN
MAKES 10–12 PIECES

COCONUT CARAMEL

1 (15-oz [420-g]) can full-fat coconut milk, liquid discarded

1 cup (200 g) coconut sugar, date sugar or packed light brown sugar

CHOCOLATE CRISPIES

½ cup (60 g) cacao powder or cocoa powder

¼ cup (60 ml) agave or other liquid sweetener

⅓ cup (80 ml) melted coconut oil

2 cups (50 g) puffed brown rice cereal

½ cup (54 g) raw slivered almonds, coarsely chopped

Flaky sea salt (optional)

Have a lined 8 x 8-inch (20 x 20-cm) baking dish nearby, oiled and lined with parchment.

To make the caramel, in a medium saucepan, whisk together the coconut cream and coconut sugar. Bring to a boil, then reduce the heat to medium and continue to cook, whisking occasionally, until the liquid condenses into a tawny pudding and reduces to one-third its volume, about 30 minutes.

To make the chocolate crispies, while the caramel is cooking, in a bowl, stir together the cacao powder, sweetener and coconut oil, until smooth. Add the cereal and almonds, and stir until completely coated. Dump half the cereal mixture into the lined dish, pressing it all the way to the edges of the pan to create a flat, even layer. Remove the coconut caramel from the stove, carefully drain away any excess oil, and then pour it over the bottom layer. Sprinkle over the last half of the cereal mixture, pressing it down to flatten. You can use a sheet of wax paper or parchment to help. Be careful because it's hot. Sprinkle with the flaked sea salt, if using, then transfer the pan to the freezer to harden before breaking into bark.

NOTE: Keep the bark in the fridge in a sealed zip-top bag for up to 2 weeks.

BLACKER BERRY CROSTADA

The blacker the berry, the sweeter the juice is in the summertime.

EGG-FREE
MAKES 2 CROSTADAS

SOUR CREAM CRUST

2 cups (240 g) whole wheat pastry flour, plus more for dusting

1 tsp salt

¾ cup (168 g) cold butter, cut into ½" (1.3-cm) cubes

10–12 tbsp (150–180 g) cold sour cream or yogurt, plus more for brushing

FILLING

3 cups (450 g) blackberries, halved

3 cups (450 g) pitted black cherries, halved

½ cup (112 g) packed brown sugar or muscovado sugar

¼ cup (30 g) white whole wheat pastry flour or other flour

1 tbsp (15 ml) vanilla extract

1 tsp orange liqueur (optional)

Raw sugar, for sprinkling

To make the crust, in a mixing bowl, stir together the flour and salt, then toss in the cubes of cold butter to coat. Using your thumb and index finger, squish the pieces of butter to flatten, and continue to break the butter up until 50 percent of the butter is crumbly, but not completely uniform in texture; you want there to be chickpea-size nuggets of butter still present. Add the cold sour cream, a few tablespoons (45 g) at a time, mixing and gathering the mixture with your hands until a shaggy dough is formed. You may not need all the sour cream. Divide the dough in half, shape the halves into 2 disks, wrap them in plastic wrap and refrigerate for at least 1 hour, or 30 minutes in the freezer. While the dough is chilling, prepare the filling.

To make the filling, in a large mixing bowl, combine all the filling ingredients and let them marinate.

Preheat the oven to 425°F (220°C or gas mark 7), and have 2 baking sheets lined with parchment nearby.

Remove one dough from the fridge, unwrap it and roll it out on a lightly floured surface into a ⅛-inch (3-mm)-thick round about 12 inches (30.5 cm) in diameter. Fill the middle with half the filling mixture and some of the juices. Fold up the edges of the pie onto itself to create a 2-inch (5-cm)-thick border. Brush the top of the crust with sour cream and sprinkle on the raw sugar. Place the pie in the freezer for 10 minutes to harden while you prepare the second crostada the same way. Place it in the freezer to chill for 10 minutes also, then bake the crostadas in the oven for 20 to 25 minutes, or until the edges turn golden brown and the fruit starts to break down into a thick syrup. Remove from the oven, allow to cool for 10 minutes, then slice and serve.

Whenever I made rice crispies with my ma, we always made them in this big, blue stockpot—the same one we'd use to make stews and soups. It was the biggest pot we had, and even though there were only five of us, we'd make enough to feed a classroom. We'd heat the butter 'til it puddled, add the bags of marshmallows, and keep stirring with a long spoon until there was a sticky mass of fluff. Then I'd dump in the cereal. Afraid everything would harden into a rock before it was time, my little arm would start mixing with panic, until the soft crackling of the puffed rice folding into the sugar would soothe me. I've made variations of this inspired by some of my favorite flavors.

RICE CRISPIES

20 MINUTES OR LESS, GLUTEN-FREE, EGG-FREE, VEGAN OPTION
MAKES NINE 3-INCH (7.5-CM) SQUARES

BOURBON BROWN BUTTER RICE CRISPIES

½ vanilla bean

2 tsp (10 ml) vanilla extract

1½ tsp (8 g) salt

2 tbsp (30 ml) bourbon

6 tbsp (84 g) unsalted butter

1 (10-oz [280-g]) bag marshmallows (vegan)

3 cups (105 g) puffed brown rice cereal

BOURBON BROWN BUTTER RICE CRISPIES

Have a 9 x 9-inch (23 x 23-cm) baking dish lined with parchment and sprayed with cooking spray nearby.

Using the tip of a knife, split the vanilla bean in half lengthwise on one side, open the bean, and then, using the back of the knife, scrape out all the seeds. Add the seeds to a small bowl along with the vanilla extract, salt and bourbon and set aside.

In a large pot, melt the butter over medium heat. Allow to cook, stirring constantly, until the butter browns, 3 to 6 minutes. Once the butter gets up to temperature, it browns quickly, so be sure to watch it.

As soon as the butter turns a golden brown color, remove it from the heat, and carefully stir in the vanilla and bourbon mixture. It will splatter a bit. Once the bubbling settles, place the pan back over the heat and dump in the marshmallows, stirring with a wooden spoon until the marshmallows melt completely. Add the cereal, folding gently to combine, and then, working quickly before the mixture stiffens, transfer it to the prepared baking dish, packing the mixture into the pan with a sheet of parchment or wax paper to make an even and dense layer. Allow to cool completely to harden, about 30 minutes, then slice into nine 3-inch (7.5-cm) squares and serve.

(continued)

RICE CRISPIES (CONT.)

Sweet Potato Rice Crispies

3 tbsp (42 g) butter

¼ cup (60 g) pureed sweet potato (about 1 small sweet potato)

1 tbsp (15 ml) vanilla extract

1 tsp salt

1½ tsp (4 g) ground cinnamon

¼ tsp ground nutmeg

⅓ cup (50 g) toasted pecans, chopped

1 (10-oz [280-g]) bag marshmallows (vegan)

6 cups (210 g) brown rice cereal

Chocolate Peanut Butter Rice Crispies

3 tbsp (42 g) butter

6 tbsp (90 g) natural peanut butter

½ cup (87 g) semisweet chocolate chips

½ tsp salt

1 tbsp (15 ml) vanilla extract

1 (10-oz [280-g]) bag marshmallows (vegan)

3 cups (105 g) puffed brown rice cereal

Sweet Potato Rice Crispies

Have an 8 x 8-inch (20 x 20-cm) or a 9 x 9-inch (23 x 23-cm) baking dish lined with parchment and sprayed with cooking spray nearby.

In a large pot, melt the butter over medium heat, then add the pureed sweet potato, vanilla, salt, cinnamon, nutmeg and toasted pecans. Add the marshmallows and continue to cook, stirring with a wooden spoon, until the marshmallows are melted. Add the cereal, folding gently to combine, and then, working quickly before the mixture stiffens, transfer it to the prepared baking dish, packing the mixture into the pan with a sheet of parchment or wax paper to make an even and dense layer. Allow to cool completely to harden, about 30 minutes, then slice into nine 3-inch (7.5-cm) squares and serve.

Chocolate Peanut Butter Rice Crispies

Have a 9 x 9-inch (23 x 23-cm) baking dish lined with parchment and sprayed with cooking spray nearby.

In a large pot, melt the butter over medium heat. Add the peanut butter, chocolate chips, salt, vanilla and marshmallows, stirring to melt. Once the chocolate and marshmallows are melted, add the cereal, folding gently to combine. Working quickly before the mixture stiffens, transfer it to the prepared baking dish, packing the mixture into the pan with a sheet of parchment or wax paper to make an even and dense layer. Allow to cool completely to harden, about 30 minutes, then slice into nine 3-inch (7.5-cm) squares and serve.

NOTES: Traditional rice crispie cereal won't hold up to the weight of the sweet potato or peanut butter versions. Be sure to use a hearty brown rice cereal. Keep the finished rice crispies in the fridge or a cool place to harden and get extra chewy.

VEGAN OPTION: Make sure the marshmallows are vegan, and made using a seaweed jelling agent instead. Be sure to use dairy-free butter or virgin coconut oil if you don't mind the tropical note it brings. For the chocolate peanut butter rice crispies, make sure the chocolate chips are dairy-free but are still able to melt.

ALMOND COCONUT CROISSANTS

I love the sound of a flaky croissant, made up of sheets of rolled dough crisped by trapped sheets of butter, and full of pockets of air when I handle them and eat them. But my eyes almost fell out of their sockets after reading through the recipes for making them. Fold this, and roll that, and chill this, so much to get that sound and texture at home. I'm a simple to please girl with a bit of a heavy hand, so I changed tradition around a lot, breaking many rules, causing uproars perhaps, but I still got away with a simple recipe that brings me back to mornings strolling the cobblestones of Rome with my sketchbook in one hand and a butter pastry in the other. And that's all I need.

VEGAN
MAKES ABOUT 14 CROISSANTS

CROISSANTS

1¼ cups (295 ml) warm water, heated to 120°F (49°C)

½ cup (100 g) coconut sugar or granulated sugar, divided

1 (2½-tsp [9-g]) packet active dry yeast

3½ cups (420 g) white whole wheat flour

½ cup (120 ml) warm oat or nut milk

1 tsp salt

1⅔ cups (385 g) coconut oil, at room temperature, divided

To make the croissants, in the bowl of a stand mixer with a dough hook attachment, combine the warm water and ¼ cup (50 g) of the sugar. Sprinkle over the yeast, and let it bloom until foamy, 5 to 10 minutes.

Add the flour, remaining ¼ cup (50 g) of sugar, milk and salt and beat on low speed until combined. As soon as all the flour is almost mixed in, mix in ⅓ cup (80 g) of the coconut oil. Turn the mixer on medium speed and knead until the dough no longer sticks to the sides of the bowl, 3 to 4 minutes. Transfer to a clean oiled bowl, cover with plastic wrap and leave it to rise for 2 hours, or until doubled in size.

Punch down the risen dough to release the air. On a lightly floured surface, roll out the dough to the size of a piece of printer paper, wrap in plastic wrap and refrigerate for 1 hour. Remove from the fridge, and smear the remaining 1⅓ cups (305 g) of coconut oil evenly over the middle third of the dough, then fold over the two edges to cover the oil. Wrap the dough in plastic wrap and place in the fridge for 1 to 2 hours to chill the coconut oil.

Remove the dough from the fridge and roll it out into an 8 x 24-inch (20 x 61-cm) rectangle, fold the rectangle in thirds, then roll it out again into an 8 x 24-inch (20 x 61-cm) rectangle. Do this 5 times, letting the dough rest on the counter so the glutens in the flour relax if it gets too difficult to roll out. It's okay if the cold coconut oil pierces the dough in a few spots. Then wrap again in plastic wrap and refrigerate for 6 to 8 hours, or overnight.

(continued)

ALMOND COCONUT CROISSANTS (CONT.)

FILLING

¼ cup (60 ml) cold oat or nut milk

½ cup (100 g) coconut sugar or granulated sugar

1 tbsp (8 g) cornstarch or arrowroot starch

⅓ cup (75 g) coconut oil

½ tsp almond extract

1 tsp vanilla extract

2 cups (240 g) almond meal flour

⅓ cup (45 g) sliced, slivered or ground almonds, for topping

⅓ cup (27 g) shredded sweetened coconut, for topping

To make the filling, whisk the milk, sugar and cornstarch together in a small saucepan over medium-low heat. Continue to whisk until thick, 2 to 3 minutes. Then add the coconut oil, almond extract and vanilla extract, whisking until combined. Stir in the almond flour, transfer to a bowl and let cool in the fridge overnight along with the croissant dough.

Have 2 half sheet pans lined with parchment nearby.

Remove the dough and filling from the fridge. Unwrap the dough and roll it out on a lightly floured work surface, into a long ¼-inch (6-mm)-thick rectangle, making sure the rectangle gets no wider than 9 inches (23 cm) across. If you need to cut the dough in half for it to fit on the work surface, that's fine, just keep the other half wrapped in the fridge while you work. Cut long triangles up the width of the rectangle that are about 5 inches (12.7 cm) across at the base. Roll 2 tablespoons (30 g) of the filling into a coil, and place it at the base of the triangle. Pull on the ends of the triangle gently to stretch them, then using your palm, press down and roll the triangle up onto itself. Place it on the baking sheet with the tip tucked under the bottom of the pastry. Cover it with plastic wrap, and continue until all the pastries are rolled. You should get about 14 croissants. Let them rise again for 1 to 2 hours, or until doubled in size.

Preheat the oven to 425°F (220°C or gas mark 7) and place a rack in the lower upper part of the oven and another in the upper lower part of the oven.

Uncover the croissants, sprinkle them with the sliced almonds and flaked coconut and bake for 20 to 22 minutes, or until puffed and browned on top and completely cooked though. Serve warm or at room temperature.

APPLE WALNUT CRUMBLE

This is the way you can have an apple pie with barely any effort and even more crunch. The flour in the crumble absorbs the fat from the butter and then the sugar caramelizes and hardens around the flour, making something as dense and crunchy as a granola to bite down on. I pile on a tall layer filled with walnuts, and that beside the soft, cinnamon-laden chunks of sweet baked apples is pure pleasure.

EGG-FREE, VEGAN OPTION, GLUTEN-FREE OPTION
MAKES ONE 9 X 9-INCH (23 X 23-CM) CRUMBLE

APPLE FILLING

3 Granny Smith apples, peeled, cored and cut into chunks

Juice of 1 lemon

½ cup (112 g) butter or virgin coconut oil

¾ cup (165 g) packed brown sugar

2 tsp (5 g) ground cinnamon

1 tsp salt

CRUMBLE TOPPING

¾ cup (90 g) white whole wheat flour

2 tbsp (26 g) granulated sugar

¼ tsp salt

¾ cup (105 g) toasted walnuts, chopped

3 tbsp (42 g) softened butter, or virgin coconut oil

Your favorite ice cream, for serving (dairy-free if desired)

Preheat the oven to 350°F (180°C or gas mark 4), position a rack in the center of the oven and have an oiled 9 x 9-inch (23 x 23-cm) baking dish nearby.

To make the filling, toss the apples and lemon juice together in the prepared baking dish. Melt the butter in a medium saucepan over medium-high heat and stir in the brown sugar. Cook for 3 to 5 minutes, or until the sugar starts bubbling and turning thick. Stir in the cinnamon and salt. Pour the mixture over the apples, tossing to coat.

To make the topping, in a bowl, toss together the flour, granulated sugar, salt and walnuts, and then work in the softened butter until the mixture is clumpy and well dispersed. Mound the mixture on top and bake in the oven for 30 to 40 minutes, or until the apples get tender and the crumble turns golden brown. Serve warm with a scoop of cold ice cream.

ALTERNATIVE FLOURS: You can use spelt flour, oat flour, rolled oats, all-purpose gluten-free flour or unbleached all-purpose flour.

ALTERNATIVE NUTS: Pecans, almonds or peanuts.

NOTE: Top the apple crumble with white chocolate chips for a pop of creamy sweetness.

COFFEE ALMOND CRUMB CAKE

I bought my first Italian coffeemaker no more than three years ago because it reminded me of mornings in Italy. In the mornings, I find myself listening to the way the boiling water bubbles on the bottom of the canister. It spits through the freshly ground espresso, up into the slotted spindle and pours out into the top of the pot. The lid lifts lightly from all the pressurized steam and then falls back down. It does this over and over again, creating a gentle "tap tap tap." It's the sound of a new morning and a fresh start.

EGG-FREE, VEGAN OPTION
MAKES ONE 9-INCH (23-CM) BUNDT CAKE

COFFEE SWIRL

½ cup (112 g) packed brown sugar or coconut sugar

1 tbsp (4 g) instant ground coffee powder

3 tbsp (18 g) shaved chocolate or mini chocolate chips

ALMOND STREUSEL TOPPING

1 cup (120 g) almond meal

⅓ cup (50 g) roughly chopped raw almonds

4 tbsp (56 g) unsalted butter, melted, or virgin coconut oil

1 tbsp (4 g) instant ground coffee powder

1 tbsp (8 g) ground cinnamon

½ tsp salt

CAKE

½ cup (112 g) unsalted butter, softened, or ½ cup (112 g) virgin coconut oil, at room temperature

¾ cup (150 g) granulated sugar

2 tsp (10 ml) vanilla extract

¾ cup (180 ml) brewed coffee, at room temperature

¾ cup (180 g) plain yogurt (dairy-free if desired)

1½ cups (180 g) white whole wheat flour

1 cup (120 g) almond meal

1 tbsp (8 g) baking powder

1 tsp salt

Cocoa nibs, for topping (optional)

Ice cream for serving (optional)

Preheat the oven to 350°F (180°C or gas mark 4) and have a 9-inch (23-cm) Bundt pan with a removable bottom nearby.

To make the coffee swirl, in a small bowl, combine the brown sugar, coffee powder and shaved chocolate; set aside.

To make the streusel topping, mix together the almond meal, chopped almonds, butter, coffee powder, cinnamon and salt in a bowl until clumpy. Set aside.

To make the cake, cream the butter, granulated sugar and vanilla in a large mixing bowl with a hand mixer, or in a stand mixer with a paddle attachment, until fluffy, about 3 minutes. In a second bowl, stir together the coffee and yogurt. In a third bowl, sift together the flour, almond meal, baking powder and salt, then fold the flour into to the creamed butter mixture in 2 batches, alternating with the coffee-yogurt mixture until just combined.

Pour half the batter into the baking dish, spreading it evenly on the bottom of the dish. Sprinkle over the swirl mixture, and then pour the other half of the cake batter on top, smoothing to even. Sprinkle over the streusel topping. Bake for 45 to 50 minutes, or until a toothpick inserted into the center of the cake comes out clean. Place a sheet of aluminum foil over the cake if the streusel starts to get too brown. Remove from the oven and allow it to cool for a few minutes. Sprinkle with the cocoa nibs, if using. Best served warm or at room temperature.

VEGAN OPTION: Be sure the chocolate chips are dairy-free, as well as the ice cream for serving.

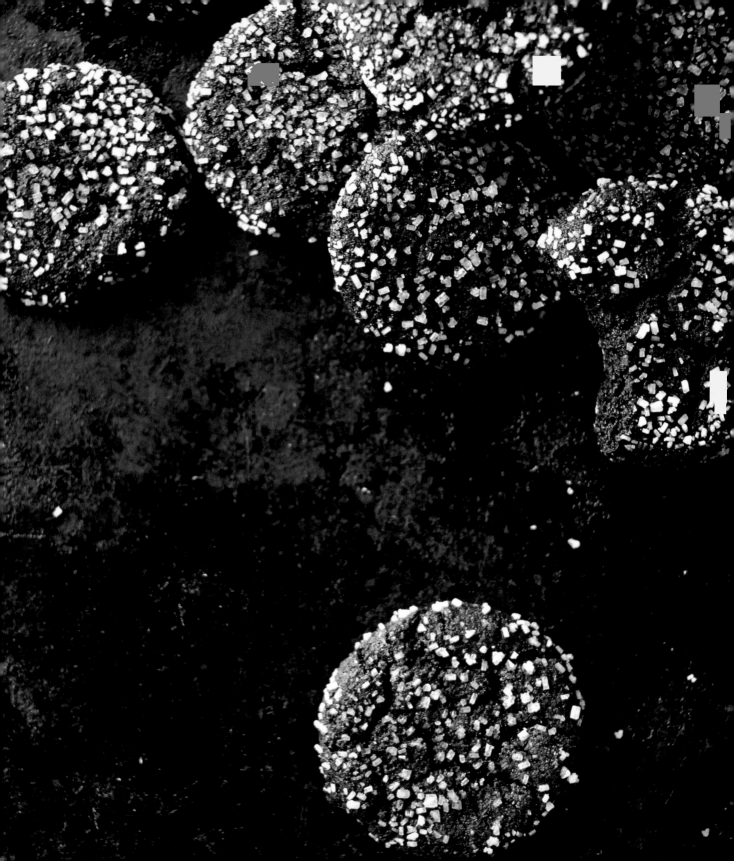

COCOA GINGERSNAP COOKIES

It'd be a shame not to celebrate the glorious SNAP of a gingersnap. The sound that resonates in your jaw toward the back of your skull. I spent a chunk of my childhood so obsessed with that sound. I'd finish off a whole bag, sometimes in under an hour.

20 MINUTES OR LESS, EGG-FREE, VEGAN OPTION
MAKES 30 COOKIES

6 tbsp (84 g) softened butter or virgin coconut oil

1 cup (200 g) granulated sugar

2 tsp (10 ml) vanilla extract

1 tsp packed fresh grated ginger

1 tsp packed orange zest

⅓ cup (80 g) flax egg (see page 30)

3 tbsp (60 g) unsulfured molasses

1½ cups (180 g) white whole wheat flour

½ cup (60 g) cacao powder or cocoa powder

2 tsp (5 g) baking soda

2 tbsp (12 g) ground ginger

1 tbsp (8 g) ground cinnamon

1 tsp salt

Sugar in the raw, for rolling

Preheat the oven to 375°F (190°C or gas mark 5). Position 2 oven racks in the center of the oven, and have 2 baking sheets lined with parchment nearby.

In a large mixing bowl with a hand mixer or in a stand mixer with a paddle attachment, cream the butter, granulated sugar, vanilla, grated ginger and orange zest until very fluffy, about 3 minutes. Then slowly add the flax egg and molasses and continue to beat until creamy. Sift in the flour, cacao powder, baking soda, ground ginger, cinnamon and salt and continue to beat until just combined. Let the batter sit for 10 minutes.

Roll 1-inch (2.5-cm) balls of dough in your palms, and then into the raw sugar to coat. Place the cookies on the baking sheet with about 2 to 3 inches (5 to 7.5 cm) between each one, and bake for 15 to 20 minutes, or until cooked and crispy. Remove from the oven and allow to cool for 5 minutes, and then transfer to a wire rack to cool completely, at least 1 hour, best overnight uncovered, before eating so they make a snap.

NOTE: It's important to let these cookies cool for a while or overnight if you can, to amplify the sound of its break.

ORANGE PEEL POUND CAKE

I miss summer days at my Big Ma's house, when we'd sit in the driveway in an uncle or aunt's parked car—all four of us cousins, each propping a door open with an extended leg—peeling back the skins of the fresh oranges Granny'd bought from the man who'd ride his bike down the street selling produce. I could feel the bass from the rear speakers throbbing against my back as I'd dig my thumbnail into the navel of the fruit to puncture its peel. I'd listen over the music for the sound of the pith slowly tearing away from the fruit, I couldn't hear it and then I'd shuck away the inedible skin. If I were back there now, I'd collect those discarded peels from the backseat of the car and turn them into something good, like a glaze or a candied topping to pound cake. And so I am.

LOW SUGAR, WHOLE WHEAT
MAKES ONE 9-INCH (23-CM) LOAF

POUND CAKE

2 cups (240 g) whole wheat pastry flour

¼ tsp baking soda

½ tsp salt

¾ cup (180 g) plain Greek yogurt or sour cream

2 oz (60 ml) orange juice + 1 tbsp (10 g) orange zest

½ cup (112 g) softened butter

½ cup (100 g) pure cane sugar

2 tsp (10 g) vanilla extract

2 eggs, at room temperature

ORANGE GLAZE

1 cup (235 ml) orange juice (from about 2 navel oranges)

Peel of 1 navel orange, white piths removed

3 tbsp (36 g) pure cane sugar

Pinch of baking soda (optional)

Preheat the oven to 350°F (180°C or gas mark 4) and place a rack in the center of the oven. Spray an 8.5 x 4-inch (21 x 10-cm) loaf pan with cooking spray and line it with a 3 to 4-inch (7.5 to 10-cm)-wide strip of parchment long enough to stretch across the pan and up the sides with a little hanging over.

To make the cake, sift together the flour, baking soda and salt in a bowl and set aside. Combine the yogurt, orange juice and orange zest in another bowl and set aside.

Beat the butter, sugar and vanilla together in a large bowl with an electric hand mixer, or in a stand mixer with a paddle attachment, until fluffy. Add the eggs, one at a time, mixing until just combined before adding the next egg. Then add the flour mixture in 2 batches, alternating with the sour cream mixture. Pour the batter into the oiled loaf pan and bake for 40 to 45 minutes, or until a toothpick inserted into the center comes out clean. You can place a sheet of aluminum foil loosely over the cake toward the end while it bakes so it doesn't brown too much.

Remove the pound cake from the oven, and let it rest for at least 20 minutes before lifting it from the pan. Transfer to a wire rack to cool for at least another 10 minutes before slicing.

To make the glaze, in a saucepan, combine the orange juice, orange peel and sugar. Bring the juice to a boil, then lower the heat to a simmer and let it cook until it's reduced to half, about 10 minutes. If the syrup tastes slightly bitter, stir in a pinch of baking soda to neutralize. Drizzle the syrup over the warm pound cake and serve.

ALTERNATIVE ORANGES: In the winter, I love to use blood oranges for their ruby red color and tartness. You may need to compensate with a little more sugar if using.

BLISTERED TOMATO SHEET PIZZA

There's nothing much like the sound of vegetables and fruits blistering in the oven. Grapes and tomatoes get so hot their skins split, and their juices splatter all over the baking sheet and then immediately evaporate—"sploosh," "sploosh," "splooooosh." It's soothing and satisfying to hear, and I know that sound means they're gonna be even sweeter when time comes to eat them.

VEGAN
MAKES 12 SQUARES

CRUST

1½ cups (355 ml) water, warmed to 120°F (49°C)

1 tbsp (12 g) packed brown sugar or granulated sugar

2 tsp (8 g) active dry yeast

3 cups (360 g) white whole wheat flour, plus more if needed

3 tbsp (45 ml) olive oil, plus more for drizzling

2 tsp (12 g) salt

TOMATO SAUCE

16 oz (455 g) ripe cherry tomatoes

3–4 tbsp (45–60 ml) olive oil, plus more for drizzling

1½ tsp salt, plus more for sprinkling

Freshly ground black pepper

8 cloves garlic, minced

3 tbsp (4 g) fresh oregano leaves

½ tsp crushed red pepper flakes

1 tbsp (12 g) granulated sugar

3 tbsp (45 ml) water

Cheese, for sprinkling (optional)

To make the crust, in a stand mixer with a dough hook attachment, combine the warm water and brown sugar. Sprinkle the yeast over the top and let sit until it's foamy, 5 to 10 minutes. Add the flour, olive oil and salt, then beat on low speed for 10 minutes. The dough should pull away from the sides of the bowl but stick to the bottom of the bowl.

Liberally oil a half sheet pan (preferably dark in color) with olive oil (it should be slippery) and transfer the dough to the pan, gently stretching it to the edges of the pan. It's okay if it doesn't reach the edges completely; don't force it. Drizzle the top of the dough with a little more oil if needed, and cover loosely with plastic wrap. Put in a warm dry place until doubled in size, about 1½ hours.

Preheat the oven to 400°F (200°C or gas mark 6). To make the tomato sauce, spread the tomatoes on a sheet tray, drizzle with olive oil and sprinkle with salt and pepper. Toss to coat. Roast for 15 to 20 minutes, until the tomatoes burst and soften. Remove from the oven.

In a large deep sauté pan, heat the 3 to 4 tablespoons (45 to 60 ml) of olive oil. Add the garlic, oregano and crushed red pepper, and cook, stirring constantly, until fragrant, 2 to 3 minutes. Add the roasted tomatoes, 1½ teaspoons (8 g) of salt and granulated sugar, and cook over medium-low heat, stirring occasionally, until the tomatoes break down into a thick sauce, about 15 minutes. You can keep a lid on the pot if the sauce begins to splatter. Remove the sauce from the heat and stir in the water to loosen. Allow the sauce to cool.

Remove the plastic from the risen dough, stretch it to the edges if it isn't already, and prod all over the surface of the dough with your fingertips to dimple it and remove large pockets of air, then gently spread over the cooled tomato sauce. Cover with the same oiled plastic wrap and let rise and rest for another 30 minutes.

Preheat the oven to 500°F (250°C or gas mark 10) and position a rack in the lower middle part of the oven. Bake the pizza for 20 to 25 minutes, or until the tomato sauce absorbs a bit, and the bottom crust is crisp and golden brown. Cut into squares and eat as is or drizzle with more olive oil and sprinkle with cheese, if desired.

SUN-DRIED TOMATO AND SEED CRACKERS

These crackers are the crunchiest crackers I've ever bit into. Don't expect a flaky saltine cracker; these will give you a resounding snap, and a beautiful contrast against a creamy hummus or guac.

30 MINUTES OR LESS, VEGAN, GLUTEN-FREE
MAKES ABOUT 3 CUPS (450 G) CRACKERS

½ cup (60 g) ground flaxseeds

1 cup (235 ml) hot water

1½ cups (225 g) raw pumpkin seeds

1 cup (145 g) raw shelled sunflower seeds

Handful of fresh oregano

2 cloves garlic

½ tsp onion powder

1 tsp salt

½ cup (55 g) sun-dried tomatoes in oil, lightly drained and minced

Preheat the oven to 350°F (180°C or gas mark 4) and have a rimmed half sheet pan lined and nearby.

Add the ground flaxseeds to a large bowl with the hot water, stir and let them sit for 5 to 10 minutes to thicken. Transfer to a food processor or blender along with all the other ingredients and pulse until coarsely chopped.

Dump the mixture into the lined sheet tray, pressing down with the back of a spoon to flatten as thinly as possible; it's okay if it doesn't reach to the edges of the pan. Bake for 25 to 30 minutes, or until the pumpkin and sunflower seeds brown and get crunchy. Remove from the oven, slice into squares or your preferred shape, turn them over, spread them out on the pan and return to the oven to bake for another 15 minutes, or until the edges brown. Remove from the oven and allow to cool for at least 30 minutes, or until they harden.

NOTE: After the crackers cool completely, transfer them to a zip-top bag and keep on the counter for a week or in the fridge for 2 weeks. Wrapping them before they cool completely may cause them to soften.

ALTERNATIVE NUTS AND SEEDS: You can use sliced almonds, chia seeds, shelled hemp seeds, sesame seeds and/or poppy seeds.

TOUCH: TEXTURES AND MOUTHFEEL

I could've built an entire book around texture and mouthfeel. The feeling behind food, the emotions and sensations they impart, is the most complicated part of eating and cooking for me. I pause and take note of how a pillow-soft sweet bread pads my mouth like cotton, how custards spread like silk across my tongue, how warm cookies and then crunchy cookies, crumble. Then there's the food I touch with my hands while cooking, helping me understand how cooked or undercooked they are, or whether they've been kneaded or whipped to their correct capacity. And I don't forget the foods with curious textures that used to catch me off guard as a kid: the sliminess of my ma's sautéed okra, or the squeakiness of zucchini she'd sneak into weeknight noodle soups. Because my experience with them is so multifaceted, they leave their mark, and I can revisit the sensations and memories attached to them with ease.

BANANAS FOSTER LUMPIA

My ma brought a handful of her comfort foods with her when she moved to the States, and lumpia and banana doughnuts were my two favorites. Lumpia are crispy fried egg rolls made of rice paper that we'd stuff with cellophane noodles and ground meats—they took all day. But banana doughnuts were easier. My ma would place three ingredients in front of me—the grayish black bananas, the flour and the granulated sugar—adding a little bit of each to a mixing bowl, then mashing it with her hands until she felt it was just right. It wasn't something you could just measure—she needed to touch it. Then we'd huddle over the deep pot of oil and start scooping the banana batter off the front end of a spoon, forcing it to ball up and fall into the hot grease. They always came out crusty on the outside and creamy on the inside. Same goes for this mash-up.

VEGAN
MAKES 8 CIGARS

LUMPIA

8 sheets whole wheat or regular phyllo dough, defrosted

2 bananas

½ cup (112 g) packed light brown sugar or coconut sugar

1 tbsp (8 g) ground cinnamon

1 tbsp (15 ml) water, nut or oat milk

1 tsp vanilla extract

½ tsp salt

½ cup (120 ml) neutral oil or dairy-free butter, melted

SYRUP GLAZE

2 tbsp (30 ml) rum

2 tbsp (30 ml) water

¼ cup (60 ml) agave or honey

¼ cup (35 g) toasted chopped macadamia nuts, for topping

To make the lumpia, unwrap the defrosted phyllo dough, lay it out on the countertop and cover with a sheet of plastic wrap and place a damp cloth on top to make sure they don't dry out while you're working. Preheat the oven to 400°F (200°C or gas mark 6) and have a sheet pan nearby.

Cut the bananas in half lengthwise, and then widthwise so you have 4 equal pieces that are about 4 inches (10 cm) long. Add them to a bowl along with the brown sugar, cinnamon, water, vanilla and salt. Toss everything gently, rubbing the bananas a little so the mixture starts to cling to them.

Lay a sheet of phyllo out on a work surface. Brush the top lightly with some of the oil, then fold the sheet in half widthwise. Rotate the sheet so the shorter end is facing you, then brush the surface again with more oil. Place a banana and some of the brown sugar mixture on the bottom middle part of the phyllo sheet, leaving about 1 inch (2.5 cm) of space from the edge. Fold up the bottom flap over the sliced banana, and then fold in the sides. Brush the top of the folded pieces with more oil, and then roll the banana up tightly to create a little egg roll shape. Place seam-side down on the sheet pan. Do this for the remaining 7 lumpia, and then bake in the oven for 12 to 15 minutes, or until golden brown and some of the filling bubbles out of some of the lumpia.

To make the glaze, combine the rum, water and agave in a saucepan, bring to a boil, cook for 1 minute, then reduce the heat to a simmer. When ready to serve, pour over the cooked lumpia and sprinkle with the toasted nuts.

TIP: Let the box of phyllo dough defrost completely in the fridge overnight to make sure it's ready to use. This step ensures the sheets won't crack.

HONEY HALVA AND CARDAMOM BISCOTTI

Finding warmth in the middle of a cold city can be a challenge. When I first moved to Boston, I struggled to make connections with people and find the type of social comfort I needed to feel settled. This is a recipe inspired by a coffee date with a new friend. We shared the drink of the day, which was coffee sweetened with honey and halva candy, and then sprinkled with ground cardamom. I've found that just like biscotti, your disposition can soften in the right company.

EGG-FREE, DAIRY-FREE
MAKES ABOUT 12 BISCOTTI

BISCOTTI

½ cup (100 g) granulated sugar
½ cup (120 ml) honey
½ cup (125 g) tahini
½ cup (120 ml) vegetable oil
¼ cup (60 ml) nut or grain milk
1 tsp vanilla extract
3 cups (360 g) white whole wheat flour
1½ tsp (6 g) baking powder
2 tsp (4 g) ground cardamom
½ tsp salt

Sesame seeds, for sprinkling
Raw sugar, for sprinkling

GLAZE

⅓ cup (80 g) coconut butter
2 tbsp (30 ml) canned coconut milk or evaporated milk
1 tbsp (15 ml) agave or honey
2 tsp (10 ml) vanilla extract

Preheat the oven to 275°F (140°C or gas mark 1) and have a lined half sheet pan nearby.

To make the biscotti, in a large mixing bowl with a handheld beater or in a stand mixer with a paddle attachment, beat the granulated sugar, honey, tahini, vegetable oil, milk and vanilla until combined. Then add the flour, baking powder, cardamom and salt, and beat until just combined.

Divide the dough in half and shape into two ¾-inch (2-cm)-tall, 4-inch (10-cm)-wide loaves on the baking sheet, leaving a couple inches (5 cm) of space between the loaves. Sprinkle them with the sesame seeds and raw sugar, and bake for 25 minutes, or until they turn light golden brown. Remove from the oven and, using a serrated knife, gently slice the loaves into 1-inch (2.5-cm)-wide cookies. Tip the cookies on their sides and place back in the oven to bake for another 20 minutes, or until the edges of the cookies turn golden brown. Remove from the oven and allow to cool, preferably overnight on the counter uncovered.

To make the glaze, in a saucepan, heat the coconut butter, coconut milk, agave and vanilla until liquefied. Allow the mixture to cool slightly, then pour into a squeeze bottle with a small tip, and drizzle over the cooled biscotti. Sprinkle with more sesame seeds, if you like.

NOTE: The cookies last for at least 2 weeks in a zip-top bag on the counter, just be sure to let them cool completely before storing or the residual heat can steam and soften the cookies.

CHOCOLATE COOKIES

I was never a fan of Double Stuf Oreo cookies, because I was the girl who'd scrape the icing out of the center of her Oreo anyway. The icing would disrupt the way the cookie would dissolve in my mouth after being saturated with milk. So because I can help it, I'll get it out of the way now.

EGG-FREE, GLUTEN FREE, 30 MINUTES OR LESS, VEGAN OPTION
MAKES ABOUT 24 COOKIES

1½ cups (180 g) almond meal or hazelnut meal

½ cup (60 g) cacao powder or cocoa powder

¾ tsp baking soda

¼ tsp baking powder

½ tsp salt

¾ cup (150 g) sugar in the raw or granulated sugar

½ cup (112 g) unsalted butter, at room temperature, or virgin coconut oil

½ tsp vanilla extract

Preheat the oven to 350°F (180°C or gas mark 4), and have a lined baking sheet nearby.

In a bowl, sift together the almond meal, cacao powder, baking soda, baking powder and salt.

In a separate bowl with an electric handheld beater or with a stand mixer with a paddle attachment, beat the sugar, butter and vanilla until fluffy. Add the dry ingredients to the creamed butter and sugar, continuing to beat on low until combined.

Roll 1-inch (2.5-cm) pieces of the dough between your palms and place on the baking sheet, pressing down into ¼-inch (6-mm) flat disks, and bake for 10 to 12 minutes, or until puffed and cooked through. Remove from the oven and let rest for at least 10 minutes, then transfer to a wire rack to cool completely before dissolving in a cup of cold milk. These cookies are delicate and crumble nicely.

TIP: Use Hershey's Special Dark cocoa powder for a dark, Oreo-like color.

TOFU CHOCOLATE CHIP COOKIES

I used to lose my enthusiasm for eating silken tofu after watching the way it'd jiggle coming out of the package, or after feeling it slush around like Jell-O in my mouth. While I squirmed, I still felt the pressure to eat it when I searched for solid sources of protein. But then I learned how well it mixes up into a batch of my favorite chocolate chip cookie dough. Cookies are the perfect place to hide it, and ironically, the edges on these come out extra crispy.

VEGAN, WHOLE WHEAT
MAKES ABOUT 24 COOKIES

1 cup (120 g) white whole wheat flour

½ cup + 3 tbsp (90 g) whole wheat pastry flour

½ tsp baking soda

½ tsp salt

1 cup (180 g) chopped dairy-free bitter and semi-sweet chocolate, plus more for topping

1 cup (240 ml) room temperature virgin coconut oil

¾ cup (140 g) granulated sugar

¾ cup (140 g) packed dark brown sugar

2 tsp (10 ml) vanilla extract

½ cup (125 g) pureed silken tofu (about ¼ of a 1-lb [500-g] package)

Sea salt flakes, for sprinkling

In a bowl, mix the flours, baking soda, salt and chopped chocolate chips together. Set aside.

In a separate bowl, with a handheld mixer, cream the coconut oil and sugars together until fluffy, about 2 minutes. Add in the vanilla and blended tofu and continue to beat until combined. Add in the flour mixture to the creamed coconut oil and sugar and, on low speed, mix until incorporated. Refrigerate for at least 30 minutes or overnight.

When ready to bake, heat the oven to 375ºF (190ºC or gas mark 5). Line a baking sheet with parchment and scoop golf ball-sized mounds of dough onto the baking sheet, leaving about 2 inches (5 cm) of space between each cookie. Insert extra chips into the top of the cookie mounds and sprinkle each cookie with the sea salt flakes. Bake the cookies for 8 to 10 minutes or until they are just browned around the edges and a little golden on the top. They will have lacey edges and should be slightly undercooked. Remove from the oven to cool slightly before eating.

BREAK N' DROP CHILE CHOCOLATE CHIP COOKIES

My sister used to be the queen of slice-n-bake cookies, except by the time we caught a good cookie rhythm, the new slice-n-bake turned to more of a break-n-drop. We'd buy frozen bricks of cookie dough that were served on a flimsy piece of cardboard, and my sister would break off one square at a time, and cook them in the toaster oven. She was also a thirteen-year-old twig, and didn't mind waiting for her food. Sometimes she'd even put them in there and forget about it, letting the edges blacken and the center dry out. When it was my turn, though, I'd conjoin two or three squares of dough, molding them into a freakish loop, and arrange them on a sheet tray. Minutes later I was in mega-cookie heaven. I'd stand at the edge of the kitchen counter waiting, watching the orange coils in the toaster heat my cookie. Most of the time I couldn't wait, though, and I'd pull the tray out too early, when it was still a little undercooked and pale in the center. That's the only way I take my cookies now, and also with a little chile powder and flaky sea salt, because I'm grown. These cookies have a widespread and addictively crunchy edge!

EGG-FREE, WHOLE WHEAT
MAKES 24 COOKIES

2¼ cups (270 g) white whole wheat flour

1 tsp baking soda

½ tsp salt

1 cup (225 g) softened butter or virgin coconut oil

1 cup (225 g) packed light brown sugar

¾ cup (140 g) granulated sugar

2 tsp (10 ml) vanilla extract

½ cup (120 ml) flax eggs

2 (3.5-oz [100-g]) bars chile chocolate, chopped

½ cup (88 g) semisweet chocolate chips

Flaky sea salt, for sprinkling

Chile powder, for sprinkling

Have a lined 9-inch (23-cm) square container with a lid for storing the cookies nearby.

In a bowl, mix together the flour, baking soda and salt. Set aside.

In a separate bowl with a handheld mixer or in a stand mixer with a paddle attachment, cream together the softened butter, sugars and vanilla until fluffy. Slowly add the flax egg, beating until combined. Add the flour mixture, beating on low speed until thick. Fold in the chopped chocolate and chocolate chips, saving some for topping.

Transfer the dough to the lined container pressing it down evenly to shape, and sprinkle on more chocolate chips, pressing them lightly into the dough, and then sprinkle on the salt and chile powder. Score the dough into 25 squares and place in the freezer until ready to bake.

Preheat the oven to 375°F (190°C or gas mark 5). Break off as many squares of the dough as you like and place them on a lined baking sheet, leaving about 2 inches (5 cm) around each cookie. Bake for 10 to 12 minutes, or until the cookies are just browned around the edges and a little golden on top. It should be slightly undercooked. Remove from the oven and transfer to a wire rack to cool slightly before eating.

NOTE: Make sure the chile powder is plain chile powder and not mixed with other spices—cumin and garlic powder are delicious and all, but not here.

HASHED COOKIES

The first job I ever had was at a café where I got to sell oatmeal chocolate chip cookies bigger than my hand. I dreamed of working in a place where I was surrounded by rows of fresh baked pastries and steamy coffee every day. The line would be out the door in the morning and I'd sneak a cookie for myself before we'd even open. They were crumbly when they were warm because I think they were made up of more pulsed oats and chocolate than flour. I'd just work my way through one, breaking little pieces off at a time to plop into my mouth, letting it dissolve on my tongue. They were the best.

VEGAN, WHOLE WHEAT, 30 MINUTES OR LESS
MAKES 9 EXTRA-LARGE COOKIES OR 18 REGULAR COOKIES

½ cup (87 g) dairy-free semisweet chocolate chips

1 cup (80 g) old-fashioned rolled oats

½ cup (70 g) toasted pecans, walnuts or hazelnuts

½ cup (112 g) organic virgin coconut oil or softened butter

¾ cup (180 g) packed brown sugar or muscovado sugar

¼ cup (50 g) granulated sugar

2 tsp (10 ml) vanilla extract

¼ cup (60 g) flax eggs (see page 30)

1 cup (120 g) white whole wheat flour or spelt flour

1 tsp baking soda

½ tsp salt

Preheat the oven to 375°F (190°C or gas mark 5) and position 2 oven racks in the center of the oven; have 2 baking sheets lined with parchment nearby.

In a food processor or blender, pulse the chocolate chips and oats into a coarse meal. Add them to a bowl. Pulse the nuts until coarsely chopped and add them to the bowl too. Set the bowl aside.

In a separate bowl with a hand mixer, or in a stand mixer with a paddle attachment, cream the coconut oil, brown sugar, cane sugar and vanilla. Then add the flax egg and beat until completely combined.

In a medium bowl, stir the flour, baking soda and salt together, and then mix it into the butter and sugar mixture until just combined. Fold in the pulsed nuts, oats and chocolate.

Using a large ice cream scooper, scoop the batter onto the lined baking sheets, leaving at least 2 inches (5 cm) between each cookie. Press the cookies down slightly and bake for 8 to 12 minutes, or until puffed and golden brown on top, but slightly undercooked in the middle. Transfer to a rack to cool slightly before eating so they hold their shape.

BAKED HALVA PRALINES

I first tasted halva, the crumbly sesame seed paste candy, after moving to the Northeast. I bought a container of the stuff (swirled with chocolate) from a Russian market down the stretch of my apartment's street. It was chalky and I had to scrape at the top of it like a frozen lilly dilly, but the way it'd melt in my mouth somehow reminded me of the delicate crumble of the prahLEENS, the candies made with sugar, nuts and cream, down South. It was a challenge, but I used my oven and the thought of those textures to create a delicious candy concoction that calls for no stove top boiling of sugar, just a bowl and a baking sheet.

30 MINUTES OR LESS, DAIRY-FREE, GLUTEN-FREE
MAKES ABOUT 16 PRALINES

1 cup (200 g) sugar

2 tbsp (30 g) tahini paste

1 egg

1 tsp vanilla extract

1 tsp salt

1½ cups (225 g) roughly chopped pecans or sliced almonds

Preheat the oven to 300°F (150°C or gas mark 2) and have a rimmed cookie sheet lined with parchment nearby.

In a bowl with an electric hand mixer or in a stand mixer with a paddle attachment, cream the sugar and tahini until crumbly and completely incorporated. Beat in the egg, vanilla and salt until combined, and then fold in the chopped nuts. Drop spoonfuls of batter onto the baking sheet, leaving at least 2 inches (5 cm) between each cookie because they spread, and bake for 22 to 25 minutes, or until browned and toasted. Transfer the cookies to a rack to cool completely and harden, about 15 minutes, and then serve.

ALTERNATIVE NUTS: You can use chopped walnuts, slivered or sliced almonds, or shelled pistachios.

ROSKETTI (CHAMORRO COOKIES)

My mother used to crush handfuls of swirled shortbread cookies, the ones from those Christmas cookie tins, into the bottom of a small cup with cold milk, creating a type of cookie slurry pudding. I realized later after having rosketti, a popular cookie from back in Guam where she's from, where that habit came from. These traditional cookies are made with an entire package of cornstarch, making anyone eating them desperate to drink up a cold cup of milk, lest they're left with an undesirable chalkiness in their mouth. I've actually cut back a little on the cornstarch even more here.

20 MINUTES OR LESS
MAKES ABOUT 24 COOKIES

½ cup (112 g) softened unsalted butter

¾ cup (150 g) sugar

2 tsp (10 ml) vanilla extract

1 egg, at room temperature

1½ cups (180 g) white whole wheat flour

1 cup (120 g) cornstarch or arrowroot starch

2 tsp (5 g) baking powder

¼ tsp salt

Preheat the oven to 350°F (180°C or gas mark 4) and position 2 oven racks in the center of the oven. Have 2 sheet pans lined with parchment and a fork for decorating nearby.

In a large bowl with a handheld beater or in a stand mixer with a paddle attachment, cream the butter, sugar and vanilla together until fluffy, 2 to 3 minutes. Add the egg and beat until incorporated. Add the flour, cornstarch, baking powder and salt, and continue to beat until combined.

Roll a 1-inch (2.5-cm) ball of dough in your palm, place it on the baking sheet and press down in the center with your thumb to create a dent. Then, using the side of the fork, press around the edges of the cookie to create a hatched design. Repeat with the rest of the cookies, and bake in the oven for 12 to 15 minutes, or until the center of the cookies puff up and they turn a light golden brown.

Remove the rosketti from the oven, transfer them to a wire rack and allow them to cool completely. Serve with a glass of cold milk.

NOTE: The cookie dough should be baked right after mixing. Letting the cookie dough rest will allow time for the starches to absorb the liquid, causing the dough to crack as you mold it.

HONEY BUNS

Corner store trips without honey bun purchases weren't worth the two-block trek. My favorite part was the quick test to make sure they weren't smashed in transit—pressing down on one inside its crinkly wrapper and waiting for it to rise back up like a saturated sponge. I'd get a whiff of pure sugar the moment I'd slide the bun out of its package—I'd grab the tail end of the roll, peel it back, the sugar coating tacking to my fingertips like Elmer's glue, and I'd plop small pieces into my mouth chased by more sugary soda. I'm baking them here for an even fluffier bun and, you'll be happy to know, with much less sugar, too.

DAIRY-FREE, EGG-FREE, WHOLE WHEAT
MAKES 11–12 BUNS

BUNS

1 cup (235 ml) nut or grain milk, warmed to 110°–115°F (43°–46°C)

¼ cup (80 g) honey

2 tsp (8 g) active dry yeast

¼ cup (60 ml) flax egg (see page 30) or 1 egg

¼ cup (60 ml) neutral oil or ¼ cup (56 g) softened butter

½ tsp salt

2 cups (240 g) white whole wheat flour

1 cup (120 g) whole wheat pastry flour

GLAZE

1 cup (120 g) confectioners' sugar, sifted

2 tbsp (30 ml) honey

3 tbsp (45 ml) milk or water

1 tsp salt

To make the buns, add the warm milk to a bowl with the honey. Sprinkle the yeast over the top and let it bloom until a cap of foam forms, 5 to 10 minutes. Pour the mixture into a large mixing bowl or the bowl of a stand mixer with a dough hook attachment, then add the flax egg, oil and salt and whisk until combined. Add the flours, 1 cup (120 g) at a time, kneading for 2 to 3 minutes or until it comes together into a ball. Transfer the dough to an oiled bowl, turning it over to coat completely. Cover it loosely with plastic wrap or a damp cloth and place it in a warm, dry place until doubled in size, about 1½ hours.

Have 2 lined sheet pans nearby. Uncover the dough and punch it down in the center to release the excess air. Pinch off 3-inch (7.5-cm) pieces of dough, and fold them over on themselves. Do this 3 times for each piece. Then roll the piece into a ball, and roll the balls into snakes that are an even thickness and 20 to 24 inches (50 to 61 cm) in length. Roll the snakes into spiral shapes, and place them on the baking sheets. Cover them again with plastic wrap or a damp cloth to rest for another 20 minutes while you make the glaze.

Preheat the oven to 325°F (170°C or gas mark 3).

To make the glaze, in a medium bowl, whisk together the sifted confectioners' sugar, honey, milk and salt until smooth. Remove the plastic from the resting buns, and gently pour the glaze over the tops of the buns, saving a little for drizzling after they come out of the oven. Cover the baking sheet loosely with foil, and bake for 25 to 30 minutes, or until the buns are puffed and just cooked through. Serve them warm with more glaze if you like.

NOTE: You can test a little yeast in a separate bowl of warm water to make sure your stash is still active before adding it to the warm milk.

LEMON RICOTTA PISTACHIO PILLOW BUNS

I took a bus to New York from Texas with less than $200 on me. I was estranged from family, broke and temporarily homeless, but those things didn't stop me from eating well; in fact, it made eating the highlight of my days. By the time I made it to New York, I sought out pasta and wine. Out came a plate arranged with plush pillows of ravioli stuffed with fluffy ricotta, bathed in lemon butter and peppered with crunchy pistachios. After walking miles with flat shoes and no real purpose, it was the comfort I lacked, and the closest thing to a warm, cozy bed I could find.

EGG-FREE
MAKES 9 BUNS

BUNS

½ cup (120 ml) milk

Zest and juice of ½ lemon

2 tbsp (30 ml) honey or agave

¾ cup (180 g) ricotta, at room temperature

1 packet (2½ tsp [9 g]) active dry yeast

1 cup (120 g) white whole wheat flour

2 cups (240 g) unbleached all-purpose flour, plus more for dusting

½ tsp salt

FILLING

½ cup (112 g) packed light brown sugar or coconut sugar

¼ cup (60 ml) olive oil

¼ cup (80 g) honey

Zest of 1 lemon

GLAZE

½ cup (112 g) cream cheese, softened

Zest and juice of 1 lemon

2 tsp (10 ml) vanilla extract

¼ cup (85 g) honey or 1 cup (120 g) sifted confectioners' sugar

⅓ cup (50 g) shelled pistachios, roughly chopped

To make the buns, add the milk to a saucepan and bring to a light simmer over medium-low heat. Do not let it boil. Add the lemon zest and lemon juice and watch the milk quickly curdle. When the curdles spread throughout the pan, remove it from the heat and stir in the honey and ricotta. Immediately add the yeast while the milk is still warm (it needs to be around 115°F [46°C]). Allow the yeast to bloom until a cap of foam is formed, 5 to 10 minutes.

In a separate bowl, combine the flour and salt. Pour in the ricotta and milk mixture and gently knead until it comes together into a rough ball. Dump onto a floured surface, and continue to knead for 5 minutes, adding a little flour here and there if the dough is too sticky to work with, but not too much or the dough will be chewy. When you're done, it should feel slightly tacky, but nothing should stick to your hands. Add the dough to an oiled bowl, cover with plastic wrap and keep in a warm place for about an hour to double in size.

To make the filling, combine the brown sugar, olive oil, honey and lemon zest. Set aside. Have an oiled 9-inch (23-cm) square baking dish nearby. Unwrap the dough, punch it down in the center to release the air, and roll it out into an ⅛-inch (3-mm)-thick rectangle on a lightly floured work surface. Spread the filling over the surface of the dough, sprinkle over the chopped pistachios and roll the dough into a log. Slice the log into 3 equal pieces, and then those pieces into 3 pieces to create 9 equal rolls. Place the rolls together in the baking dish, cover with plastic wrap and let rest for another 20 to 30 minutes, or until they've risen another 30 percent.

To make the glaze, in a bowl, whisk together the softened cream cheese, lemon zest and juice, vanilla and honey until combined. I also like to add everything to a food processor and blend until smooth. Set aside.

Preheat the oven to 375°F (190°C or gas mark 5). Bake the rolls for 30 to 35 minutes, or until the buns are puffed, golden and cooked all the way through. Remove the buns from the oven and spread on the glaze, allowing it to melt over the warm rolls, and sprinkle with the pistachios. Serve warm.

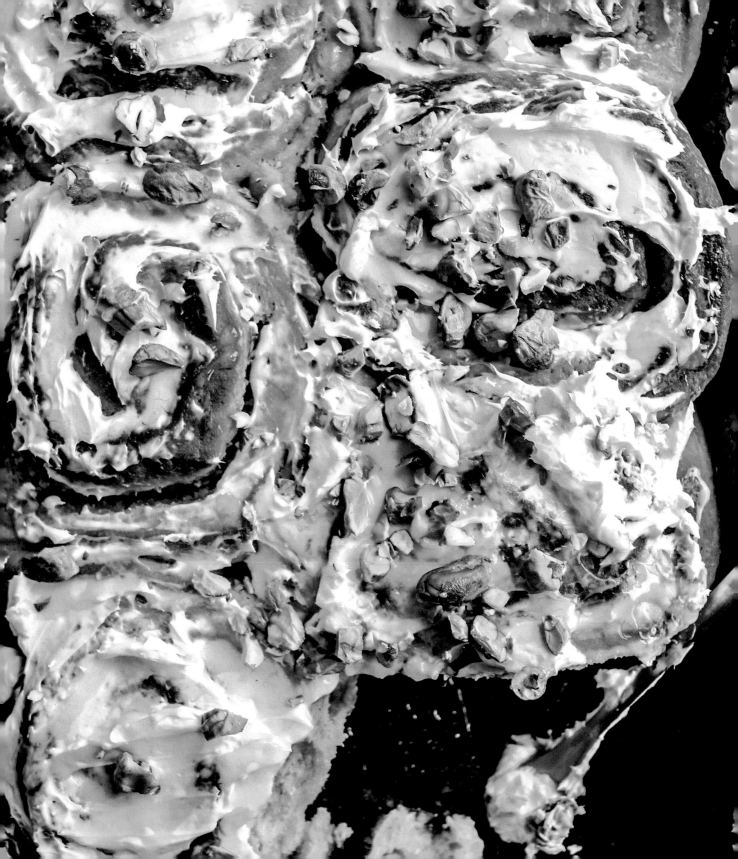

SPINACH AND FETA POCKETS

The mini hot pockets that used to blister the roof of my mouth when they came out of our toaster oven, and all the melted cheese and hot tomato sauce that would brush by it, inspired this recipe. I'm making a version packed with spinach and feta. Thankfully, these ingredients can't hurt me.

MAKES ABOUT 15 POCKETS

FILLING

1 small yellow onion, minced

2 tbsp (30 ml) olive oil

2 cloves garlic, minced

½ tsp crushed red pepper flakes

1 tsp dried oregano

1 tsp dried basil

1 tbsp dried dill

1 (10-oz [280-g]) package frozen spinach, thawed and drained of water

½ tsp salt

Juice of 1 lemon

¼ cup (60 g) ricotta or cream cheese

2 oz (56 g) feta, crumbled

CRUST

2 cups (240 g) white whole wheat flour, plus more for dusting

½ tsp salt

½ tsp baking powder

½ cup (112 g) butter, cut into cubes

1 egg or ¼ cup (60 ml) flax egg (see page 30)

1 tsp vinegar

3–4 tbsp (45–60 ml) cold water

Olive oil, for drizzling
Marinara sauce, for serving

To make the filling, in a saucepan, sauté the onion in the oil over low heat for 3 to 4 minutes, or until translucent. Add the minced garlic, red pepper flakes, oregano, basil and dill, and cook until fragrant, about 2 more minutes. Turn off the heat and fold in the drained spinach, salt, lemon juice, ricotta and crumbled feta; transfer to a bowl and place it in the fridge to cool while you make the crust.

To make the crust, in a food processor, pulse together the flour, salt and baking powder. Then pulse in the cubed butter until the size of peas. In a separate bowl, whisk together the egg, vinegar and water, and then slowly add it to the flour, pulsing just until the dough comes together into a shaggy ball. Dump the dough out onto a surface, shape into a disk and wrap in plastic wrap. Refrigerate for at least 30 minutes.

Preheat the oven to 425°F (220°C or gas mark 7) and have a baking sheet drizzled with olive oil nearby.

Remove the dough from the fridge, and roll it out on a work surface dusted lightly with flour until it's a ⅛-inch (3-mm)-thick rectangle. Cut strips from the dough that are roughly 2 x 6-inch (5 x 15-cm) and fill the strips with about 1 tablespoon (15 g) of filling on one side. Fold the other side over the filling to close, and tightly pinch the edges together. Place the pockets on a lined baking sheet, and work quickly as you continue with the remaining pieces of dough. If the dough gets warm as you work, place the tray of prepared pockets in the freezer for 10 to 15 minutes before baking. Drizzle the tops with more olive oil and bake for 8 to 10 minutes, or until puffed and golden. Serve with your favorite marinara sauce.

NOTE: The pizza pockets can be flash frozen: Spread out on a baking sheet and freeze for 1 hour, then transfer them to zip-top bags to freeze until ready to bake. Bake frozen pockets for 15 to 18 minutes.

STRAWBERRY BUTTER ROSE BUNS

My ma had a ritual when we lived in LA that had something to do with control and missing my father. She'd portion out her meals and sometimes would skip them altogether when her appetite would disappear. Her favorite breakfast was toasted white bread with some kind of pink jam, a generous schmear of margarine and a caldron of hot Lipton tea. The fat from the butter would salt and soften the bread and the strawberry jam would brighten it. Something about the fat and sugar helped neutralize her depression, and the tea would soothe her heart. I'd copy her some mornings, but I would always feel unsatisfied by the amount of space it'd take up in my stomach. I needed something more substantial. Something like a pastry.

EGG-FREE, VEGAN OPTION, WHOLE WHEAT
MAKES 12 BUNS

BUNS

¾ cup (180 ml) oat or nut milk, warmed to 115°F (46°C)

¼ cup (50 g) packed brown sugar or coconut sugar, divided

1¼ tsp (4 g) active dry yeast

1½ cups (180 g) white whole wheat flour

1½ cups (180 g) whole wheat pastry flour

½ tsp salt

¼ cup (60 g) flax egg (see page 30) or 1 egg, at room temperature

½ cup (112 g) softened butter, divided (dairy-free if desired)

½ cup (140 g) strawberry jam

3 tbsp (36 g) granulated sugar

Zest and juice of 1 lemon

STRAWBERRY GLAZE

2 strawberries, hulled

Juice of 1 lemon and zest of ½ lemon

1 cup (120 g) confectioners' sugar

To make the buns, in a bowl, add the warm milk and 1 tablespoon (13 g) of the brown sugar. Sprinkle over the yeast and let it bloom until a cap of foam forms on the top, 5 to 10 minutes.

In a large mixing bowl or stand mixer with a dough hook attachment, combine the flours and salt. Then add the bloomed yeast mixture, the remaining 3 tablespoons (37 g) of brown sugar and the thickened flax egg. Knead the ingredients until a dough is formed, about 2 minutes in a stand mixer. Once the dough has formed, add ¼ cup (56 g) of the butter and continue to knead until the butter is completely worked in and the dough is smooth and tacky. Transfer it to a clean, oiled bowl, cover it with plastic wrap and leave it in a warm dry place until it is doubled in size, about 1½ hours.

Lightly flour a work surface and a rolling pin and have an oiled muffin tin nearby. Unwrap the risen dough, punch it down in the center to release the air and roll it out to an 11 x 22-inch (28 x 56-cm) rectangle. Spread the strawberry jam and the remaining ¼ cup (56 g) of softened butter all over the surface, and then sprinkle over the granulated sugar, lemon zest and lemon juice. Starting at the wider end of the dough, cut it into 12 equal strips, then roll the strips tightly into buns. Place the buns in the oiled muffin tin, cover again with plastic wrap and let them rest for 20 to 30 more minutes.

Preheat the oven to 375°F (190°C or gas mark 5). Unwrap the buns and bake them in the oven for 18 to 22 minutes, or until puffed and golden brown on top. Remove the buns from the oven and make the glaze.

To make the glaze, in a blender, blend the strawberries, lemon juice, lemon zest and confectioners' sugar until smooth. Strain to remove the seeds, if you like, and drizzle over the warm buns. Serve.

SWEET POTATO PIE WITH CHOCOLATE HAZELNUT CRUST

Thanksgiving eve in the Guy family household was all about baking the desserts—cheesecake and sweet potato pie—for the next-day dinner so they could chill overnight. Oven space was limited, which meant roasting the sweet potatoes skipped to the front of the line. So much time went into these pies—first the roasting, then the mashing, then the baking, then the chilling; but in the end, slicing through the soft custard and arriving at the bland crust didn't give me enough satisfaction for all the work. I'd always felt the crust was too plain next to its magnificent, silky center. I'm switching the crust to a crumbly chocolate hazelnut here because my mother never liked things with cinnamon, especially her pie. This recipe doesn't use it in the filling, but I've added fresh nutmeg and orange juice to the mixture and more nutmeg to the surface of the pie to highlight the subtle flavors of the sweet potato. One-fourth of a fresh grated nugget is perfect.

GLUTEN-FREE, DAIRY-FREE
MAKES ONE 9-INCH (23-CM) PIE

FILLING

4–5 medium sweet potatoes or yams

½ cup (120 ml) nut or oat milk

3 eggs

½ cup (112 g) packed brown sugar

2 tsp (10 ml) vanilla extract

Zest and juice of ½ an orange

⅛ tsp freshly ground nutmeg

¼ tsp salt

CRUST

2 cups (240 g) hazelnut meal flour

2 tbsp (28 g) coconut oil or butter, divided

½ cup (87 g) dairy-free semisweet chocolate chips

¼ tsp salt

Preheat the oven to 400°F (200°C or gas mark 6).

To make the filling, clean the sweet potatoes and, using a fork or paring knife, carefully poke holes into the potatoes to create air pockets. Place on a baking sheet and roast them for 45 to 50 minutes to allow the natural sugars to caramelize slowly. Check the doneness by pressing down on them with an oven mitt; they should cave. Remove them from the oven and allow them to cool completely, then peel off and discard their skins.

Lower the oven temperature to 300°F (150°C or gas mark 2) and have a 9-inch (23-cm) springform pan nearby.

To make the crust, in a skillet, slowly toast the hazelnut flour over low heat, stirring constantly so it doesn't burn, 4 to 5 minutes. Once the hazelnut flour begins to take on a popcorn scent, turn off the heat and add the oil, chocolate chips and salt. Continue to stir until the chocolate is melted and completely incorporated. Dump the hazelnut mixture into the bottom of a springform pan, and press the mixture down evenly and 1 inch (2.5 cm) up the sides. You can use the bottom of a cup if your hands are sensitive to the heat.

Continue with the filling by blending the milk, eggs, brown sugar, vanilla, orange juice and zest, nutmeg, salt and peeled and cooled sweet potatoes in a blender or food processor until completely smooth. Pour the filling over the crust.

Place the pie in the oven on the upper middle rack and bake for 45 to 50 minutes, or until the center is set. Remove from the oven and allow it to cool slightly and then refrigerate it for a few hours or overnight. Slice and serve with whipped cream, if you like.

ZUCCHINI BREAD

I remember asking my mom what those translucent chunks of food were that were showing up in her pots of chicken soup. "It's zucchini squash," she'd say, and I'd stare into the pot with confusion, wondering how it turned from green to clear. So she started letting me prep the zucchini so I could witness its transformation from the beginning. I remember the first time I tried to chop it. I felt my fingers slip and squeak along surface of the squash's meat. And just like back then I still find myself squirming, like I'm hearing squeaking Styrofoam, when I touch its flesh.

EGG-FREE, VEGAN OPTION, WHOLE WHEAT
MAKES ONE 9 x 5-INCH (23 x 12.7-CM) LOAF

½ cup (112 g) unsalted butter, softened (dairy-free if desired)

½ cup (100 g) sugar

2 tsp (10 ml) vanilla extract

½ cup (120 g) unsweetened applesauce, at room temperature

¼ cup (60 ml) honey

2 cups (240 g) white whole wheat flour

1 tsp baking powder

1 tsp baking soda

1 tsp salt

¾ cup (180 ml) oat or nut milk, at room temperature

Zest and juice of 1 lemon

1 cup (120 g) shredded zucchini, squeezed of its liquid

Cinnamon sugar for topping, optional

Preheat the oven to 425°F (220°C or gas mark 7), and position a rack in the upper middle part of the oven. Spray a 9 x 5-inch (23 x 12.5-cm) loaf pan with cooking spray and line it with a 4-inch (10-cm)-wide strip of parchment long enough to stretch across the width and up the sides with a little hanging over.

In a large bowl with a handheld beater or in a stand mixer with a paddle attachment, cream the butter, sugar and vanilla until fluffy, 2 to 3 minutes. Stir together the applesauce and honey, and slowly pour it into the creamed butter and sugar, continuing to beat until smooth.

Sift the flour, baking powder, baking soda and salt into a separate bowl. In a third bowl, stir the milk and lemon zest and juice together, and allow a few minutes to curdle.

Folding gently, add the flour mixture to the bowl of creamed butter and sugar in 2 batches, alternating with the milk and lemon juice mixture. Just as it comes together, fold in the drained zucchini, being careful not to overmix. Pour the batter into the prepared loaf pan, smoothing the top, and bake for 35 to 40 minutes, or until a toothpick inserted into the center comes out clean. Remove the bread from the oven and let it rest for 10 minutes before lifting it from the pan. Transfer to a wire rack to cool for at least another 10 minutes. Top with cinnamon sugar if you like, then slice and serve.

NOTE: You can replace half or all of the shredded zucchini with equal amounts of shredded drained apples.

KOMBUCHA MUFFINS

I'm obsessed with kombucha, the fermented tea drink. I drink it like I used to drink soda as a kid: at least once a day. I crave the feeling of that cold, carbonated liquid hitting my chest, giving me the sensation it's opening my lungs for the first time that day . . . it's addicting. I love watching the agitated bubbles rise to the lip of the bottle, too. I can tell it's going to be a gusher when the cap is bulging before I even open the bottle. I thought I could use the carbonation and acid to make some kind of quick bread or breakfast muffin. So this is my tea-twist on the Irish soda bread I come across so often here in Boston.

20 MINUTES OR LESS, EGG-FREE, VEGAN OPTION, WHOLE WHEAT
MAKES 12 MUFFINS

3 cups (360 g) white whole wheat flour or spelt flour

4 tsp (10 g) baking soda

½ tsp salt

½ cup (112 g) unsalted butter, melted, or neutral oil

¾ cup (180 ml) agave or honey

1 (16-oz [470-ml]) bottle plain kombucha

Preheat the oven to 425°F (220°C or gas mark 7). Oil the wells of a muffin tin and have it nearby.

In a large bowl, stir together the flour, baking soda and salt. Pour the melted butter and agave over the dry ingredients, and then pour in the kombucha. Whisk the mixture until just combined. Don't overmix or your muffins will be tough.

Immediately divide the mixture among the muffin wells, and bake in the oven for 5 minutes. Then reduce the oven temperature to 375°F (190°C or gas mark 5) and finish cooking for another 8 to 10 minutes, or until a toothpick inserted into the center of a muffin comes out clean. The initial high heat of the oven will make sure the muffins pop out over the edges of the pan. Remove from the oven and allow to cool slightly. Serve warm with more softened butter, if you like.

ALTERNATIVE FATS: You can use melted dairy-free butter or a neutral oil like grapeseed, safflower, sunflower or canola oil.

ORANGE JUICE AND OLIVE OIL BREAD

Was every American household split between pulp-lovers and pulp-haters? It sometimes feels that way. Me? I always voted for the cartons with a little pulp, because feeling the small bits of the orange fruit tickling the sides of my mouth as I swallowed a glass of juice made me feel like the juice was fresh.

WHOLE WHEAT, DAIRY-FREE
MAKES ONE 9 x 5-INCH (23 x 12.7-CM) LOAF

2 cups (240 g) white whole wheat flour

1 tsp baking powder

½ tsp baking soda

¾ tsp salt

½ cup (120 ml) olive oil

¾ cup (150 g) sugar

2 tsp (10 ml) vanilla extract

2 eggs

1 cup (235 ml) orange juice with pulp

Zest of 1 orange

Preheat the oven to 375°F (190°C or gas mark 5). Oil a 9 x 5-inch (23 x 12.5-cm) loaf pan and line it with a 4-inch (10-cm)-wide strip of parchment long enough to stretch across the width and up the sides with a little hanging over.

In a bowl, stir together the flour, baking powder, baking soda and salt. Set aside.

In a large bowl, whisk together the olive oil, sugar, vanilla, eggs, orange juice and orange zest until combined. Sift in the dry ingredients, then fold until just combined. Pour the batter into the loaf pan and bake for 35 to 40 minutes, or until a toothpick inserted into the center comes out clean. You can cover the pan loosely with foil if it is getting too brown. Remove the pan from the oven, and let the bread rest for at least 20 minutes before lifting the bread from the pan. Transfer to a wire rack to cool for at least another 10 minutes, then slice and serve.

OPTIONAL GLAZE: I love the crunchy crust of this loaf of bread, but if you want to garnish it with icing, whisk together 1 cup (120 g) of sifted confectioners' sugar with ½ cup (120 ml) of orange juice and 1 teaspoon of Grand Marnier or other orange liqueur (optional). Pour it over the cooled, unsliced bread, let it harden then slice and serve.

I remember summertime days in Alabama, being little, watching Big Ma sit at a round, low-rise, wooden table with her sister, the both of them talking mess while they prepped a bowl of okra for frying. She'd cut the tops off the raw okra by just holding one in her hands, pressing her thumb against the top and cutting up against her thumb with a paring knife, as if her thumb were a cutting board. I'd think about how thick her skin must've been for it to be able to come up against the edge of a blade without getting sliced open. Then I'd watch her as she'd bread and fry her okra to mask the sliminess from the starch inside. I've found that pairing it with something equally as gooey, like melted cheese, makes the texture just as easy to swallow.

SMOKED OKRA DIP

EGG-FREE, GLUTEN-FREE
MAKES 2 CUPS (480 G)

8 okra pods

2 tbsp (30 ml) olive oil, plus more for drizzling

1 shallot, diced

½ tsp crushed red pepper flakes

Salt and pepper, to taste

1 (8-oz [228-g]) package cream cheese, softened

⅓ cup (80 g) plain nonfat Greek yogurt

2 tbsp (28 g) mayonnaise (optional)

1 tsp mild hot sauce

¾ cup (90 g) shredded smoked Gouda, divided

½ cup (60 g) shredded mozzarella

Paprika, for sprinkling

Preheat the oven to 400°F (200°C or gas mark 6) and have two 8-ounce (228-g) ramekins or one 16-ounce (455-g) ramekin nearby.

Trim the tops off the okra and slice them in half lengthwise and then again in half widthwise. Set them aside.

In a medium sauté pan over medium-high heat, heat the olive oil. Add the diced shallot, cooking until it softens a bit, about 3 minutes, stirring often. Add the crushed red pepper flakes, the quartered okra and salt and pepper to taste. Cook, stirring often, for another 3 to 4 minutes, or until the okra begins to soften slightly. Remove from the heat and set aside.

In a large bowl, combine the cream cheese, yogurt, mayonnaise (if using), hot sauce, ½ cup (60 g) of the smoked Gouda, mozzarella and more salt and pepper to taste. Fold in the cooked okra and shallots, and then transfer the mixture to the ramekins. Sprinkle the tops with the remaining ¼ cup (30 g) of Gouda and paprika and bake for 10 to 12 minutes, or until the cheese melts and the top gets a little crusty. Serve warm with your favorite chips. I like blue tortilla chips.

GRITS AND GREENS SOUFFLÉ

To make a pot of collard greens, I rip the ribs from the center of the leathery leaves, then stack them like dollar bills, roll them like cigars and slice through them like an onion. I stuff them into a deep pot, listening to them crackle and sizzle when they touch the hot bottom, and in a moment, watch them shrink to moss, leaving me room to pile more greens into the pot. In goes the seared ham hock or turkey leg (when I used to cook with them) and always vinegar and a big pinch of sugar to round out the bitterness. It's a habit that we make too much, so there's still the pot sitting on the stove when breakfast comes and we can serve it up alongside creamy cheese grits and freshly fried fluffy eggs. The saucy greens slurp up well when mixed into the grainy grits.

MAKES FOUR 8-OZ (228-G) SOUFFLÉS

2 tbsp (30 ml) olive oil

4 oz (112 g) collard greens, fresh or frozen, cleaned and chopped

Pinch of sugar (optional)

Salt and crushed red pepper flakes, to taste

1 tbsp (15 ml) white wine vinegar or other vinegar

¾ cup (180 ml) water

⅓ cup (95 g) stone-ground grits

2 tbsp (28 g) butter

2 tbsp (16 g) flour

1 cup (235 ml) milk

⅓ cup (40 g) shredded cheddar cheese (optional)

4 eggs, at room temperature, separated

¼ tsp cream of tartar

Preheat the oven to 350°F (180°C or gas mark 4) and position an oven rack in the middle of the oven. Have four 8-ounce (228-g) ramekins, arranged on a baking sheet, buttered and dusted lightly with flour, nearby.

In a medium saucepan, heat the oil and add the chopped collard greens, sugar, if using, and salt and red pepper flakes to taste and cook until the collard greens soften, 3 to 4 minutes. Deglaze the pan with the vinegar and continue to cook for another minute, then transfer the collards to a plate or bowl and set aside.

In the same saucepan, bring the water to a boil. Whisk in the grits, season with salt and lots of pepper and stir until thick, about 1 minute. Stir in the butter and flour, continuing to whisk for another 1 to 2 minutes, then whisk in the milk, cheese, if using, and cooked collard greens, and stir until combined. Remove the pan from the heat and set aside to cool slightly. Once it's cooled, stir in the egg yolks, whisking until completely combined.

In a clean metal bowl, combine the egg whites and cream of tartar and beat with a hand mixer until stiff and glossy peaks form. Fold one-third of the whipped egg whites into the cooked grits, and then add all the grits to the whites, folding gently until just combined, being careful not to deflate the whites.

Spoon the mixture into the ramekins, leaving ¼ inch (6 mm) from the top. Run a butter knife around the edges to create the extra puffed layer on top. Place the ramekins on a baking sheet, place the baking sheet on the bottom rack of the oven and cook until puffed and jiggly, 20 to 25 minutes. Serve immediately out of the oven alongside a fresh, lemony salad.

NOTE: If you use frozen collards, be sure to thaw and then drain them before adding to the recipe.

TASTE: SPICE, HEAT AND FLAVOR

I take great pride in my crowded spice cabinet. Rows and stacks and buckets and bags stuffed with spices I've gathered from trips and stores or ordered online. Whenever I think about making anything, I first imagine the different spices mingling together in my head in a web pattern. What works with what? I ask. Then I spend a good twenty minutes combing through the mass of flavors I've collected to find them. Spices bring boldness to some of my favorite dishes, and I'll always be fascinated with them, but I also find myself trying to enhance or highlight simple flavors too, those imparted from fresh fruit or vegetables or more subtle, overlooked ingredients. Sometimes when the spices are too heavy they can ruin elements of the dish, and so it's fun to seek out the perfect balance.

MAQUE CHOUX STRATA

Louisiana was a place where I witnessed my father get treated like a king for the first time in my life. On our summer road trips we would stop there to sleep in the whitest sheets I'd ever seen. Nine-year-old me wanted to stay forever because life there tasted as rich as the food we'd eat. Mother's and Daughter's famed breakfast biscuits; beignets that would leaves stamps of confectioners' sugar somehow entangled in the curls of my hair; thick, soul-coating gumbo. Even the corn was done up, cooked with sweet red peppers and creamy butter. It didn't taste like any corn we'd ever had. But it's easy to bring that same rich flavor with me and add it to other dishes, because I can find those simple ingredients anywhere.

SERVES 4–6

2 tbsp (28 g) butter or olive oil

1 small yellow onion, diced

½ tsp crushed red pepper flakes

5 sprigs of thyme

3 cloves garlic, minced

1 red bell pepper, cored, seeded and diced

1 cup (140 g) fresh or frozen corn kernels

Salt and pepper, to taste

4 eggs

1 cup (235 ml) milk

4–8 dashes of hot sauce

3 cups (150 g) cubed day-old baguette or toast

Paprika, for sprinkling

Chopped parsley, for garnish

In a large sauté pan, heat the butter over medium-high heat and add the onion. Cook for 3 minutes, or until tender, and then add the red pepper flakes, sprigs of thyme and minced garlic and cook until the garlic begins to perfume, 1 to 2 minutes. Add the red pepper, corn kernels and salt and pepper to taste. Reduce the heat to medium and cook, stirring occasionally, until the red peppers begin to soften, another 6 to 8 minutes. Remove from the heat and set aside.

Have an oiled 9-inch (23-cm) casserole dish with lid nearby. In a mixing bowl, whisk together the eggs, milk and hot sauce, and season with salt and pepper to taste. Whisk in the cooked vegetables, and then dump in the cubed bread, tossing to coat completely. Press down on the bread to help it absorb the liquid, and then transfer it to the oiled casserole dish. Sprinkle with paprika and chopped parsley, cover the dish with the lid and let it sit in the fridge to continue to soak for at least 30 minutes; you can even leave it overnight.

Preheat the oven to 425°F (220°C or gas mark 7).

Remove the casserole dish from the fridge and bake the strata, with the lid on, for 35 to 40 minutes, or until the bread is toasted, puffed and cooked through.

NOTE: Aluminum foil can sub in for a lid.

FIVE-SPICE COCONUT RICE PUDDING

Unsurprisingly, I first stumbled on the effluvious Chinese five-spice powder in Chinatown in Boston. One of my favorite restaurants off of Tyler Street seasoned their syrup with the complex spice to spill over warm egg waffles. Ever since then, I've been fascinated by the mix of fragrant clove, the crushed peppercorns that add woodsy heat and the sharp licorice notes from the star anise and fennel. Together the spices create a smooth, pungent flavor that I'm starting to think should be used more often to embolden cinnamon-heavy classics, like rice pudding, one of my favorites.

Vegan
Serves 8–12

2 (15-oz [420-g]) cans full-fat coconut milk

6 tbsp (90 ml) Grade A or B maple syrup

2 tsp (10 ml) vanilla extract

½ tsp sea salt

½ cup (90 g) jasmine rice

1 cinnamon stick

1–2 tsp Chinese five-spice powder, to taste

Preheat the oven to 350°F (180°C or gas mark 4).

In a saucepan, bring the coconut milk, maple syrup, vanilla and salt to a simmer.

Add the rice to a casserole dish, and pour the hot coconut milk over the top, stirring to coat the grains. Add the cinnamon stick, cover the dish with aluminum foil and bake for about 1 hour, or until the rice is creamy and cooked through. As it bakes, you'll hear the sound of the bubbling coconut milk, and the dancing rice as it hits the top of the foil.

Remove the pudding from the oven and sprinkle the top with the five-spice powder to taste. Remove the cinnamon stick and serve warm or chill.

MANGO LIME COCONUT CAKE

I miss the tropical flavors of Florida, the tangy Key limes, the fallen coconuts drying out underneath our neighbor's palm trees and the saccharine smell of overripe mangoes. We'd buy a couple of containers of mango meat from the 45th Street flea market and they'd be soaked in lime juice and coated in cayenne pepper. Munching on the marinated spears, we'd stroll through the market staring up at the hanging mannequins dressed in FUBU and all the latest trends, and pass by all men and women gathering inside the open barbershops and braiding salons. That was usually how we'd spend a Saturday.

EGG-FREE, VEGAN OPTION, WHOLE WHEAT
MAKES A THREE-LAYERED 8-INCH (20-CM) CAKE

MANGO LIME CAKE

1⅓ cups (305 ml) nut or grain milk

Zest and juice of 2 limes

1 cup (225 g) softened unsalted butter, or room temperature virgin coconut oil

2 cups (400 g) sugar

1 tbsp (15 ml) vanilla extract

1½ cups (355 g) mango puree, at room temperature

3 cups (360 g) white whole wheat flour

1 tbsp (8 g) baking soda

1½ tsp salt

1½ cups (120 g) shredded coconut

Preheat the oven to 350°F (180°C or gas mark 4) and position 2 racks in the center of the oven. Have three 8-inch (20-cm) cake pans oiled and their bases lined with parchment nearby.

To make the cake, in a small bowl, combine the milk, lime zest and lime juice and let it sit until curdled, about 3 minutes.

In a large mixing bowl with a handheld beater or in a stand mixer with a paddle attachment, cream the softened butter, sugar and vanilla until smooth and fluffy. Add the room temperature mango puree, ¼ cup (60 g) at a time, continuing to mix until it's completely combined.

In a medium bowl, combine the flour, baking soda and salt. Gently fold the dry ingredients into to the mango mixture in 2 batches, alternating with half the milk, being careful not to overmix (a few clumps of flour in the batter is fine). Fold in the coconut. Divide the batter among the 3 cake pans, smoothing out the top, and bake them for 25 to 30 minutes, or until golden brown and a toothpick inserted into the center comes out clean.

Remove the cakes from the oven, transfer them to a wire rack, and allow to cool completely before icing, at least 1 hour. If you are making this a day in advance, let the cake come to room temperature, then wrap it in plastic wrap and keep it on the counter until you're ready to ice it.

(continued)

MANGO LIME COCONUT CAKE (CONT.)

To make the mango mousse icing, combine the mango puree, sugar, salt and lime zest in a small saucepan over medium heat. Cook for a few minutes, until the sugar dissolves, then whisk in the tapioca. Cook, whisking constantly so the bottom doesn't burn, until the mixture is very thick, 3 to 5 minutes. Transfer the mixture to a bowl, and place it in the fridge to allow it to cool completely so it doesn't heat the whipped cream.

When it's time to assemble the cake, finish the mousse: in a large mixing bowl, beat the whipped cream until soft peaks form, then slowly drizzle in the cooled mango mixture, and beat on high speed until stiff peaks form.

For a multilayered cake, slice the cooled cakes through the center before icing, otherwise place one cake upside down on a cake stand, add one-fourth of the whipped mousse on top, smooth it out almost to the edges with an offset spatula and then top with another mango cake turned upside down. Add another one-fourth of the mousse and smooth to the edges. Add the final cake on top and add the rest of the whipped mousse on top, creating divots and peaks with the back of the spatula. Garnish with the mango slices and serve.

Mango Mousse Icing

½ cup (120 g) mango puree

½ cup (100 g) sugar

1 tsp salt

Zest of 1 lime

2 tbsp (16 g) tapioca flour

2½ cups (588 ml) cold heavy cream

Fresh mango slices, for topping

VEGAN OPTION: Replace the heavy cream by chilling two 15-ounce (420-g) cans of full-fat coconut milk (preferably Thai Kitchen brand) overnight, then open the cans upside down and drain away the coconut water that has separated from the cream. Scoop out the coconut cream and proceed with the recipe.

COCONUT LEMONGRASS MERINGUE WITH GINGERBREAD CRUST

Key limes are everywhere in South Florida, and the tart pies we used to make with them are a part of my blood. But those zesty limes are so hard to come by up north, and when I don't have something as special and punchy as a Key lime, my instinct isn't to replace it with something as common as a lime, but instead something equally as special and accessible. Asian markets have replaced the Latin markets I grew up next to, and that's why and when I stumbled on the flavor of lemongrass. It marries well with coconut, too.

VEGAN, WHOLE WHEAT
MAKES ONE 9-INCH (23-CM) TART

Gingerbread Graham Cracker Crust

2 cups (240 g) white whole wheat flour

1 cup (120 g) golden flax meal or graham flour

½ cup (100 g) granulated sugar

¾ tsp salt

1 tbsp (7 g) ground ginger

1 tsp ground cinnamon

½ tsp salt

½ cup (112 g) coconut oil or butter, melted

¼ cup (80 g) molasses

Filling

4 stalks lemongrass

2 (15-oz [420-g]) cans full-fat coconut milk

1 cup (200 g) granulated sugar

Zest and juice of 1 lime

3 dried kaffir lime leaves

1 tbsp (15 ml) vanilla extract

½ tsp salt

6 tbsp (60 g) cornstarch

3–4 tbsp (45–60 ml) cold water

Preheat the oven to 350°F (180°C or gas mark 4) and have an oiled 9-inch (23-cm) tart pan on a baking sheet nearby.

To make the crust, combine all the ingredients in a bowl and then press into the bottom of the prepared tart pan. Bake for 10 to 15 minutes, or until it begins to perfume and the top darkens slightly. Remove from the oven and allow it to cool.

To make the filling, if you're using fresh lemongrass, cut off and discard the bottom stems and the tough upper part of the stalk, then remove any tough outer leaves. With the handle of a large knife, bang against the stalk to release the oils. Add the stalks to a large saucepan along with the coconut milk, granulated sugar, lime zest and juice, lime leaves, vanilla and salt. Bring it to a boil, reduce the heat to a simmer and cook for 10 minutes, or until slightly reduced. Strain the liquid to remove the bits of lemongrass, then add the liquid back to the pan. In a small bowl, whisk the cornstarch together with the water until completely combined and then add it into the saucepan. Cook, whisking continuously, until thick, about 5 minutes. Pour the mixture into the cooled tart pan and chill in the fridge for 4 hours or overnight, until ready to serve.

(continued)

COCONUT LEMONGRASS MERINGUE WITH GINGERBREAD CRUST (CONT.)

When you're ready to serve, preheat the oven to 350°F (180°C or gas mark 4) and place an oven rack in the upper part of the oven, about 7 inches (17.8 cm) away from the coil.

To make the meringue, in a clean stand mixer with the whisk attachment, beat the aquafaba and cream of tartar on high speed until soft fluffy peaks form, 3 to 4 minutes. Slowly add the superfine sugar, beating continuously until the mixture turns stiff, 5 to 6 minutes. Add the vanilla and beat until incorporated. Dollop the mixture on top of the chilled pie, and using the back of a spoon, create textural peaks. Place it in the oven to brown, 10 to 12 minutes, watching it carefully to make sure it doesn't burn. Remove the meringue from the oven, slice and serve.

Aquafaba is the liquid brine from a can of chickpeas or legumes. A 15-ounce (420-g) can has about ¾ cup (180 ml) of aquafaba. Save the chickpeas or legumes and use them in a salad or other dish later on.

Egg-Free Meringue
⅔ cup (160 ml) aquafaba*

¼ tsp cream of tartar

1 cup (130 g) superfine sugar

1 tsp vanilla extract

QUINOA BANANA BREAD MUFFINS

Road trips were the highlight of my daddy's summer, and he'd put all his money into them because it meant he'd be back with his family in Mississippi again. Our family of five would ride from the southern part of Florida up and across the panhandle and into Shelby, Mississippi, stopping as little as possible. He wouldn't stop at all if he could help it, but usually me or my sister slowed him down, begging to pee, and so he'd pull over to a gas station. We'd scatter to the restroom, and he'd stop by the counter to buy a soft banana bread muffin. Nowadays, when I find him eating things like this, knowing he shouldn't, I experiment with a homemade version, sneaking in more nutritious ingredients and waiting for his reaction to see if he can taste the difference. Most times he can't.

GLUTEN FREE, VEGAN
MAKES 12 MUFFINS

2 cups (240 g) quinoa flour

4 ripe bananas

¾ cup (150 g) coconut sugar or packed brown sugar

½ cup (120 ml) neutral oil

1 cup (235 ml) oat or nut milk

2 tsp (10 ml) vanilla extract

½ tsp banana extract (optional)

¾ cup (90 g) almond flour

4 tsp (10 g) baking powder

½ tsp salt

½ cup (72 g) toasted walnuts, chopped

If you can, toast the quinoa flour. See the note below.

Preheat the oven to 425°F (220°C or gas mark 7), and have an oiled standard muffin tin nearby. I like to 86 the muffin holders because they can obstruct the domed shape I'm looking for.

In a blender or food processor, blend the bananas until liquefied. Transfer to a large mixing bowl and mix in the coconut sugar, oil, milk, vanilla and banana extract, if using.

In a separate bowl, combine the quinoa flour, almond flour, baking powder, salt and walnuts. Fold the dry ingredients into the wet ingredients, being careful not to overmix, and divide the batter among the oiled muffin wells. Bake them in the oven for 8 minutes, then turn the heat down to 375°F (190°C or gas mark 5) and continue baking for 15 to 18 minutes, until a toothpick inserted into the center of a muffin comes out clean.

TIP: If you want your muffins to have a pretty bubbled top like the ones in the packages, the oven temperature must be fairly hot when they first go in. After 8 minutes of baking, lower the temperature to cook them all the way through.

NOTE: These muffins use quinoa flour, which has a strong and sour taste from the natural saponins in the plant; they're good for you, but can taste a bit like soap. I highly recommend toasting the flour in the oven at 300°F (150°C or gas mark 2) for 30 to 40 minutes until the smell disappears. It'll soften the final flavor. Remove from the oven and allow it to cool completely, then proceed with the recipe, and no one will ever know.

CHOCOLATE, CHOCOLATE VENEER CAKE

I don't have a big taste for icings, especially sugar-saturated ones that are dense. For the most part, I like my cakes unembellished, served underneath a dollop of cold whipped cream. Hand me my cupcake with a swirl of buttercream taller than the cake itself, and I will scrape 95 percent of it off and into my napkin. I'm sure I got this attitude from my mother, who wasn't into decorated cakes either. She craved simple devil's food cake, baked from the box, warm, with a large scoop of nearly melted vanilla ice cream. She kept an army of those boxes in the house with only half as many containers of chocolate frosting. I decided to keep this icing fluffy, cold, thin and just sweet enough.

EGG-FREE, VEGAN OPTION
MAKES ONE 9-INCH (23-CM) LAYER CAKE

CHOCOLATE CAKE

2 cups (240 g) white whole wheat flour

⅔ cup (160 g) cacao powder or cocoa powder

1½ tsp (6 g) baking powder

1 tsp baking soda

1 tsp salt

1¼ cups (250 g) sugar

1 cup (235 ml) buttermilk (see page 200 for vegan buttermilk)

½ cup (120 ml) neutral oil

1 tbsp (15 ml) vanilla extract

1 cup (235 ml) hot coffee

CHOCOLATE ICING

1 cup (175 g) dairy-free semisweet chocolate chips, melted

3 tbsp (42 g) coconut oil

1 (15-oz [420-g]) can full-fat coconut cream, preferably A Taste of Thai, chilled in the fridge overnight

Berries for serving, optional

Preheat the oven to 350°F (180°C or gas mark 4) and have two 8 or 9-inch (20 or 23-cm) oiled cake pans lined with parchment nearby, and place a metal mixing bowl in the freezer to get icy.

To make the cake, stir together the flour, cacao powder, baking powder, baking soda and salt in a bowl. Set aside.

In a separate bowl, whisk the sugar, buttermilk, oil and vanilla until smooth. Sift the dry ingredients into the wet ingredients, and fold them together gently to combine until almost completely blended, being careful not to overmix, then pour in the hot coffee, whisking to combine. Divide the batter between the oiled cake pans and bake for 25 to 30 minutes, or until a toothpick inserted into the center comes out clean. Remove the cakes from the oven and allow them to cool for 10 minutes, then flip them out onto a wire rack to finish cooling while you make the icing.

To make the icing, in a small cup, mix the melted chocolate and coconut oil together until silky. Let it cool to room temperature if the chocolate is still hot. Remove the coconut cream from the fridge and, being careful not to shake it, flip it upside down and then open the can from the bottom. Discard the unsolidified liquid, keeping the thick cream at the top, then scoop the thick coconut cream into the cold metal bowl. With an electric handheld beater, beat the coconut cream until fluffy, then slowly drizzle in the melted chocolate, continuing to beat until the cream gets stiff. Place the bowl in the fridge to chill for 20 minutes or until you're ready to ice the cakes.

When the cakes are completely cooled, place one of the cakes upside down on a cake stand or large serving plate so the top is completely flat. Spread one-fourth of the icing over the top, then add the other cake on top of the icing. Finish icing the top and sides with the rest of the chocolate icing. Top with fresh berries if you like and slice and serve, or place the cake in the fridge to set the icing.

STICKY MAPLE MINI CAKES

My maple syrup game has changed since childhood. Real maple syrup, not the butter-scented or candy-sweet pancake syrup I grew up on, has a complex flavor I didn't learn about until I moved north and (relatively) close to Vermont. Grade A maple has a slight malty and sometimes chicory taste, and Grade B has even more smokiness. I love them both, and have fallen out of the habit of buying the other stuff. But because the real maple syrup can be much thinner than what I was used to, I bring it to a boil on the stove top and thicken it into something more like a caramel sauce.

VEGAN
MAKES 5–10 MINI CAKES

MINI CAKES

10 pitted Medjool dates

½ cup (120 ml) evaporated coconut milk or regular evaporated milk

½ cup (112 g) dairy-free butter, softened, or virgin coconut oil

1 tsp vanilla extract

1 cup (120 g) white whole wheat flour

1½ tsp baking powder

MAPLE SAUCE

½ cup (120 ml) maple syrup, Grade A or B

2 tbsp (28 g) virgin coconut oil

1 (15-oz [420-g]) can full-fat coconut milk

1 tsp salt

2 tsp (10 ml) vanilla extract

½ cup (87 g) toasted pecans, chopped

To make the cakes, place the dates in a heatproof bowl and cover with boiling water. Give them at least 20 minutes to soften.

Preheat the oven to 375°F (190°C or gas mark 5). Oil a mini Bundt cake pan or the wells of a standard muffin tin and have nearby.

Once the dates are soft, transfer them to a food processor, leaving behind the excess water, and blend them with the evaporated coconut milk until a smooth and creamy paste is formed. If the mixture is not cooled, let it come to room temperature before continuing so the residual heat doesn't melt the butter.

In a bowl or stand mixer, beat the butter and vanilla together until creamy, and then slowly add the date paste, scraping down the sides of the bowl and beater as you go, until everything is smooth and incorporated. Fold in the flour and baking powder until just combined, being careful not to overmix. Then fill the oiled cake pan to the top, scraping off any excess batter with the back of a butter knife so the batter is flush with the edge. Bake the cakes for 10 to 18 minutes, depending on the size of the pan, or until a toothpick inserted into the center of a cake comes out clean. Remove them from the oven and allow the cakes to cool before flipping them out onto a wire rack.

To make the sauce, while the cakes are cooling, combine the maple syrup, coconut oil, coconut milk, salt and vanilla in a saucepan and bring to a boil, stirring frequently until the sauce thickens and reduces slightly, 10 to 12 minutes. Finish the sauce by stirring in the toasted pecans. Remove the sauce from the heat, and drizzle over the warm cakes to serve.

PEANUT BUTTER JELLY BREAD

I used to call my PB&Js "peanut butter–scented sandwiches." My ma would buy those already-swirled-together pinstripe jars of peanut butter and jelly and spread a good ¼ cup (60 g) onto a couple of slabs of thick-sliced potato bread. For her, the ratio of peanut butter to jelly in the jar was perfect. For me, I never liked that much peanut butter. It left my mouth tacky and dry. I would scrape a small scoop from the jar and onto the billowy-soft bread just to get a little taste, and then double the jelly, just enough to sweeten the bread, not caring that I was disrupting the jar's equilibrium. I never wanted to overpower the flavor and texture of the soft bread.

VEGAN
MAKES TWO 9-INCH (23-CM) LOAVES

1¼ cups (295 ml) warm oat or nut milk

4 tbsp (50 g) sugar, divided

1½ tsp active dry yeast

3 cups (360 g) unbleached bread flour, plus more for dusting

¾ tsp salt

¼ cup (36 g) peanut butter powder

6–8 tbsp (90–120 g) favorite jelly

NOTE: You can test a small amount of your yeast in warm water first to make sure it's still alive.

In a small bowl, combine the milk with 2 tablespoons (25 g) of the sugar, then sprinkle the yeast over the top and let it sit and bloom until a thick cap of froth is formed, 5 to 10 minutes.

In a stand mixer with a dough hook attachment, combine the flour and salt. Add the remaining 2 tablespoons (25 g) of sugar along with the bloomed yeast and peanut butter powder. Knead the mixture for 3 to 4 minutes, or until it turns into a springy dough. Place the dough in a clean oiled bowl, cover with plastic wrap and a damp cloth and place it in a warm dark place to double in size, about 60 to 90 minutes.

Lightly flour a work surface and a rolling pin and have two 9 x 5-inch (23 x 12.5-cm) oiled loaf pans lined with 4-inch (10-cm)-wide strips of parchment long enough to stretch across the width and up the sides of the pan with a little hanging over.

Unwrap the risen dough, punch it down in the center to release the air and roll it out to roughly a 16 x 30-inch (40.6 x 76-cm) rectangle. Spread the jelly all over the surface, then roll the dough up tightly from the shorter end. Slice the log in half so you have roughly two 8-inch (20-cm)-long rolls. Transfer them to the prepared loaf pans; if they're longer, compress the rolls slightly, like accordions, or tuck the ends under to fit. Cover the bread again with plastic wrap and a warm damp dish towel and keep in a dark place to double in size for another 60 to 90 minutes. The bread should peak out just slightly above the edges of the pan, or at least come up very close but not poof far over the edges.

Preheat the oven to 350°F (180°C or gas mark 4) and position an oven rack on the lower half of the oven.

Bake the loaves for 50 to 60 minutes, or until you can hear a hollow knock when you tap on the bottom of the baked loaf with your knuckle. Transfer to a wire wrack to cool for at least 20 minutes. Slice and serve with sliced banana and honey, if you like.

A POET'S PEANUT BUTTER COOKIE

I grew up hating peanut butter cookies. I never understood their appeal. But then again, I'm the same girl who made PB&J sandwiches—if you could call them that—with thin veneers of peanut butter. Why would someone crave such a crumbly, crunchy cookie? Even stranger, one with no chocolate chips? So I steered clear of them and their crosshatched symbol for so long . . . But then I went to a poetry meet-up on the outskirts of Boston and tasted the juiciest peanut butter cookie—no harrowing hatches on the top, just a cookie, perfectly chewy and tender, and stuffed with whole beans of roasted peanuts. I got a pop of nutty, smoky and salty peanut flavor and felt my poor disposition toward them melt away entirely. Chocolate chips are only optional this time.

20 MINUTES OR LESS, VEGAN, WHOLE WHEAT
MAKES 24 COOKIES

1 cup (180 g) creamy all-natural unsalted peanut butter

½ cup (120 g) room temperature virgin coconut oil

2 cups (190 g) coconut sugar

2 tsp (4 ml) vanilla extract

¼ cup (60 ml) flax eggs, at room temperature (see page 30)

1½ cups (145 g) white whole wheat flour

½ tsp baking soda

½ tsp salt

⅔ cup (120 g) roasted unsalted peanuts

Sea salt flakes, for sprinkling (optional)

Preheat the oven to 375°F (190°C or gas mark 5). Have 2 lined baking sheets nearby.

In a bowl with a handheld mixer or in a stand mixer, cream the peanut butter, coconut oil, sugar and vanilla until smooth. Add the flax egg slowly, beating until combined.

In a separate bowl, combine the flour, baking soda and salt. Slowly add the dry ingredients to the wet, mixing until just combined. Fold in the roasted peanuts, if using, and then, using an ice cream scoop, drop spoonfuls of the dough onto the prepared baking sheets, leaving 1 to 2 inches (2.5 to 5 cm) of space between each cookie. Sprinkle with the sea salt flakes, if you like, and bake for 12 to 15 minutes, or until just browned and puffed. Remove from the oven, allow to cool for 5 minutes before serving.

NOTE: For any natural peanut butter you're using, be sure to stir it well before measuring, because the oil separates as it sits. Add ½ cup (87 g) of chocolate chips if desired when folding in the peanuts.

PEPPER JELLY THUMB- PRINT COOKIES

The natural sugars in the sweet red bell pepper makes it easier for my tongue to withstand the heat from the chili flakes. It's a trick I've use in everything from the strawberry jalapeño hand pies I used to make in the summertime, to these perfectly balanced, textured shortbread cookies I make in the fall.

VEGAN
MAKES ABOUT 24 COOKIES

RED PEPPER JELLY

2 red bell peppers, seeded and cut into chunks

2 tbsp (30 ml) olive oil

1 tbsp (4 g) crushed red pepper flakes

¾ cup (150 g) sugar

5 tbsp (75 ml) apple cider vinegar

½ tsp salt

2 tbsp (15 g) pectin

CORNMEAL SHORTBREAD COOKIES

¾ cup (168 g) softened dairy-free butter or virgin coconut oil

⅔ cup (135 g) granulated sugar

½ cup (60 g) cornstarch or arrowroot starch

1 tbsp (15 ml) vanilla extract

1 tsp salt

1 cup (120 g) white whole wheat flour or unbleached all-purpose flour

1 cup (140 g) finely ground cornmeal

To make the jelly, in a food processor or blender, puree the chunks of red bell pepper until smooth. Set aside.

In a saucepan over medium-high heat, heat the olive oil and then add the crushed red pepper flakes, stirring constantly until the flakes begin to toast and turn dark brown, about 1 minute. Add the pureed red bell pepper, sugar, apple cider vinegar and salt, and bring to a boil, stirring until the sugar dissolves, about 5 minutes. Add the pectin and continue to boil until the mixture thickens slightly, 1 to 2 minutes. Let the mixture cool, and then transfer to a glass container and refrigerate for a couple hours or until thick.

Preheat the oven to 375°F (190°C or gas mark 5) and have a cookie sheet lined with parchment nearby.

To make the cookies, in a large mixing bowl with a handheld mixer or in a stand mixer with a paddle attachment, beat the butter and sugar until fluffy, about 3 minutes. Add the cornstarch, vanilla and salt, and continue to beat until combined. In a separate bowl, mix the flour and cornmeal together, and then add it to the butter and sugar mixture, beating until just combined. Pinch off 1½ to 2-inch (3.8 to 5-cm) pieces of the dough, roll them into small balls, place them on the cookie sheet, leaving about 2 inches (5 cm) of space between each cookie and press in the center of the cookies with your thumb. Fill the center of the cookies with 1 to 2 teaspoons of the red pepper jelly. Run the outside of the jelly container under hot water if you need to loosen it up after chilling.

Bake the cookies for 10 to 12 minutes, or until they are cooked through. Remove them from the oven and allow them to cool slightly, then top them off with more of the pepper jelly, because some absorbs into the cookies as they bake.

GRIDDLED CORNBREAD MUFFINS

My Big Ma would always add extra sugar and milk to boxes of Jiffy cornbread mix. It made the crumb even softer. When I would copy her they came out perfect every single time. I never had the need to make my own from scratch, until I read the nutrition label on the back. There on the box, near the top of the ingredient list, it listed "animal lard," and as a vegetarian at the time, I was brokenhearted and forced to start experimenting with a new cornbread invention.

This version is inspired by a handful of diner trips I've made across the country that served me corn muffins in the morning. One of my favorite diners on the upper West Coast offered a slew of red pepper jelly packets for slathering on top of my toasted corn muffin, and now I don't suppose there's any other way I'll do it again.

WHOLE WHEAT
MAKES 9 CORN MUFFINS

1½ cups (180 g) whole wheat pastry flour

¾ cup (128 g) finely ground cornmeal

2 tsp (5 g) baking soda

1 tsp baking powder

1½ tsp (8 g) salt

6 tbsp (84 g) softened butter, plus more for cooking

½ cup (112 g) packed light brown sugar

1 large egg, at room temperature

¾ cup (180 ml) milk, at room temperature

½ cup (70 g) corn kernels, fresh or frozen (optional)

1 tbsp (14 g) butter

Red Pepper Jelly (page 178), for serving (optional)

Preheat the oven to 425°F (220°C or gas mark 7) and position a rack in the upper middle part of the oven. Spray a standard 12-cup muffin tin with cooking spray and set it aside.

In a bowl, mix together the flour, cornmeal, baking soda, baking powder and salt. Set aside.

In another large bowl and using a handheld electric beater, cream together the butter and brown sugar until fluffy, about 3 minutes. Add the egg, beating until combined. Fold in the flour and cornmeal mixture in 2 batches, alternating with the milk, until just combined, and then fold in the kernels of corn, if using, being careful not to overmix. Transfer the batter to the oiled muffin tin, smooth the tops, bake for 5 minutes and then turn the heat down to 375°F (190°C or gas mark 5) and bake for another 8 to 10 minutes, or until a toothpick inserted into the center comes out clean. Remove the cornbread from the oven and let the muffins cool.

To griddle the cornbread, when ready to serve, melt about 1 tablespoon (14 g) of butter in a small cast-iron skillet, slice a corn muffin in half and place it cut-side down in the skillet to toast, about 1 minute. Serve with red pepper jelly, if you like.

SAFFRON SOYMILK PIE

I stopped drinking cow's milk straight a long time ago, probably when I was ten or eleven and my mom tried to limit my diet by confining me to soymilk and Boca burgers. The soymilk was strange and chalky to me at first, but I grew to appreciate the flavor. I love the smooth aftertaste—it doesn't stick so sharply in the back of my mouth or coat my tongue like I remember whole milk doing. It also adds a subtle flavor when it's mixed with other things that also have a pleasant edge of flavor, such as saffron.

EGG-FREE, VEGAN OPTION
MAKES ONE 9-INCH (23-CM) PIE

CRUST

6 sheets phyllo crust, unthawed

6 tbsp (84 g) butter, melted, or neutral oil

FILLING

2½ cups (590 ml) soymilk, or other plant-based milk

¾ cup (150 g) granulated sugar

3 tbsp (42 g) softened butter or neutral oil

⅓ cup (40 g) flour

1 tbsp (15 ml) vanilla extract

¼ cup (55 g) packed brown sugar

½ tsp salt

Big pinch of saffron threads

Lemon zest, for sprinkling

Preheat the oven to 375°F (190°C or gas mark 5) and have a 9-inch (23-cm) pie plate nearby.

To make the crust, place a sheet of phyllo dough into the pie plate. Using a pastry brush, lightly brush the top of the sheet with the melted butter. Add another layer of phyllo on top, and brush the top again. Continue until all the sheets of dough are stacked, compressing the edges to create a frilled border. Place in the freezer for 10 to 15 minutes to harden while you make the filling.

To make the filling, in a food processor or blender, combine the soymilk, granulated sugar, butter, flour, vanilla, brown sugar and salt.

Remove the crust from the freezer, fill it with the soymilk mixture, then sprinkle on the saffron threads, crushing them lightly between your fingers before letting them fall on top. Stir in the threads a little with your finger and then bake until the pie is set in the center, 60 to 65 minutes. Remove the pie from the oven and sprinkle the top with lemon zest, then let it come to room temperature. Serve it as is, or place it in the fridge to chill overnight to set up.

CARROT CAKE CHEESECAKE

My daddy can't spend a holiday without a slice of carrot cake. But then again he's a cheesecake man too, so every year we end up with both desserts, taking up extra pans, extra space in the oven and all the shelves in the fridge until the feasting was over and the food packed away. I figured that because carrot cake gets topped with cream cheese icing anyway, I could save space and time without sacrificing any of his favorite flavors.

EGG-FREE, VEGAN OPTION
MAKES 8 BARS

CARROT CAKE

⅓ cup (50 g) raisins

1½ cups (180 g) white whole wheat flour

1 cup (120 g) almond meal

2 tsp (5 g) baking powder

¼ tsp baking soda

1 tsp ground cinnamon

¼ tsp ground allspice

½ tsp salt

3 pineapple rings

2 large carrots, peeled

⅓ cup (80 ml) neutral oil

½ cup (100 g) granulated sugar

2 tsp (10 ml) vanilla extract

¼ cup (37 g) chopped toasted walnuts

CHEESECAKE LAYER

1 (8-oz [228-g]) package cream cheese, softened (dairy-free if desired)

¼ cup (50 g) granulated sugar

2 tsp (10 ml) vanilla extract

Zest and juice of 1 lemon

1 tbsp (8 g) flour

Confectioners' sugar, for topping (optional)

Preheat the oven to 350°F (180°C or gas mark 4). Oil an 8 x 4 x 1½-inch (20 x 10 x 4-cm) baking dish and line it with a strip of parchment that stretches across the width.

To make the cake, place the raisins in a bowl, cover with boiling water and let them soak for 10 to 15 minutes until plump. Drain the water and set the raisins aside.

In a medium bowl, combine the flour, almond meal, baking powder, baking soda, cinnamon, allspice and salt and set aside.

In a food processor or blender, blend the pineapple until pureed, then add to a large mixing bowl. Back in the food processor, blend the carrots until pureed like the pineapple but not liquefied. Dump the carrots into the bowl with the pureed pineapple, then whisk in the oil, granulated sugar, vanilla and rehydrated raisins. Fold in the flour mixture, being careful not to overmix, followed by the toasted nuts. Pour the batter into the prepared cake pan, smoothing the top to create an even layer. Bake for 35 to 40 minutes, or until the top is completely set, then turn the heat down to 300°F (150°C or gas mark 2).

To make the cheesecake, in a large bowl, beat the softened cream cheese, granulated sugar, vanilla, lemon zest and juice until smooth, then beat in the flour until just combined. Remove the cake from the oven and, using an offset spatula, gently spread the thin layer of cheesecake over the top of the cake, all the way to the edges of the pan, smoothing out the top. Place the cake back in the oven to bake for another 10 to 12 minutes, or until the cream cheese has set and browned on top. Remove from the oven, lift the cake from the pan, top with confectioners' sugar, if using, slice and serve.

I love this cake warm and gooey straight from the oven but it's great chilled overnight, too—if you're fortunate enough to have the extra shelf space in the fridge.

CHESTNUT SKILLET CORNBREAD

When I first moved to Rome to study there, I turned to food because I felt lost and lonely. Usually I find the urge to bake when it probably makes the least sense to do it. For instance, if you don't read Italian (let alone speak it), trying to shop in the city's market for more obscure baking supplies like baking soda or cream of tartar is going to be a challenge. Also, if the oven in the building you live in only has two temperatures, off and on, you should probably only make recipes that call for broiling and/or warming. I stumbled through a recipe intent on making cornbread like my grandmother's, but somehow invented an entirely new flavor. Note to self: *farina di castagne* is not cornmeal; it's chestnut flour.

GLUTEN-FREE, VEGAN OPTION, 30 MINUTES OR LESS
MAKES ONE 8-INCH (20-CM) CORNBREAD

1 cup (120 g) chestnut flour

½ cup (85 g) finely ground cornmeal

½ tsp salt

3 tbsp (36 g) pure cane sugar

2 tsp (5 g) baking powder

5 tbsp (75 ml) melted butter or neutral oil, divided

½ cup (120 ml) oat or nut milk

1 egg or ⅓ cup (80 g) applesauce

Preheat the oven to 400°F (200°C or gas mark 6).

In a bowl, sift together the chestnut flour, cornmeal, salt, sugar and baking powder. Set aside.

Add 2 tablespoons (30 ml) of the butter to an 8-inch (20-cm) cast-iron skillet and heat, swirling the pan to coat.

Whisk the milk, egg and remaining 3 tablespoons (45 ml) of melted butter into the flour mixture until just combined. Once the butter is sizzling, add the batter to the skillet, and then place it in the oven to bake for 20 to 25 minutes, or until a toothpick inserted into the center comes out clean. Carefully remove from the oven, slice and serve.

NOTE: The batter can also be baked as muffins.

CAJUN-RUBBED FLATBREAD

I find myself fighting my cravings for the Cajun food I grew up eating, the bold spices we'd sprinkle over seared shrimp, toss into creamy pastas or use to blacken meats and fillets of fish. I never thought of dressing warm bread in a similar way until I tried Mediterranean food and tasted a flatbread chip that had been smothered in za'atar—an herb concoction made up of Mediterranean spices and seeds like cumin and sesame. After that experience, rubbing breads with paprika, basil, cracked pepper and cayenne, and all the rich Cajun spices that peppered my past, is something I do regularly. It's a shame I hadn't thought of it sooner.

VEGAN
MAKES 4 FLATBREADS

CAJUN SPICE RUB

3 tbsp (45 ml) olive oil

2 tsp (4 g) onion powder

6 cloves garlic

2 tsp (4 g) ground cumin

2 tsp (4 g) paprika

2 tsp (4 g) chili powder

½ tsp cayenne pepper

2 tsp (2 g) dried thyme

2 tsp (2 g) dried basil

2 tsp (2 g) dried oregano

Handful of fresh chopped cilantro

1 tsp salt

1 tsp peppercorns

FLATBREAD

½ cup (120 ml) warm water

1 tbsp (12 g) sugar

2 tsp (10 g) yeast

1¾–2 cups (170–190 g) unbleached all-purpose flour, plus more for dusting

½ tsp salt

2 tbsp (30 ml) olive oil, plus more for drizzling

To make the spice rub, blend all the ingredients in a blender or food processor until combined. Set aside.

To make the flatbread, combine the warm water and sugar in a small bowl, then sprinkle the yeast over the top and let it bloom until a cap of foam is formed on the top, 5 to 10 minutes.

In a large mixing bowl, combine the flour, salt and olive oil. Pour in the yeast mixture and mix with your hands or a wooden spoon until a dough forms. Dump the dough out onto a lightly floured surface and knead for 2 minutes with your hands until the dough springs back to the touch. You can add a little extra flour or olive oil to make the dough wetter or drier as needed. Transfer to a clean, oiled bowl, cover with plastic wrap and keep in a warm place until doubled in size, 1 to 1½ hours. Remove the dough from the bowl, punch it down and divide it into 4 pieces. Roll each piece into a ball. Cover again with a damp cloth and let the dough rest for 20 minutes.

Preheat the oven to 500°F (250°C or gas mark 10) and place a sheet pan in the upper middle rack of the oven to heat.

When the dough has rested, uncover a piece of dough, drizzle it with more olive oil, and stretch it out into a 6 to 8-inch (15 to 20-cm) disk. Carefully remove the hot sheet pan from the oven and drop the dough on the pan. Bake for 5 to 6 minutes, or until puffed, slightly charred on the bottom and golden brown on the top. Remove from the oven and spread on the Cajun rub. Serve warm.

JAMAICAN-STYLE PATTY POT PIES WITH PICKLED SLAW

There are powerful spices in these pot pies that mimic the flavor of the Jamaican beef patties we'd buy from the corner store growing up. The crusts alone have such a vivid orange color, and their butteriness adds the perfect complement to the intense spices laced throughout. Careful, though, when you start making this and the fragrant spices hit the bare pan and release their oils, they might make you tear up.

VEGAN OPTION
MAKES 4 POT PIES

PICKLED CARROT CABBAGE SLAW

½ cup (55 g) shredded carrot

1 cup (100 g) shredded cabbage

½ yellow onion, thinly sliced

3 tbsp (45 ml) vinegar

2 tbsp (24 g) sugar

Leaves from 1 sprig of fresh thyme

Salt and pepper, to taste

CRUST

3 cups (360 g) whole wheat pastry flour, plus more for dusting

1 tbsp (6 g) curry powder

2 tbsp (12 g) ground turmeric

1 tsp salt

1 cup (225 g) very cold unsalted butter or virgin coconut oil

1 egg or ¼ cup (60 ml) flax egg (see page 30)

2 tbsp (30 ml) apple cider vinegar

½ cup (120 ml) ice cold water

To make the slaw, combine all the ingredients in a bowl and let it sit and pickle for at least 30 minutes. The slaw becomes more flavorful the longer it sits.

To make the crust, in a large bowl, combine the flour, curry powder, turmeric and salt. Toss the cold butter cubes into the flour using your hands, flattening them and crumbling them into the flour until the mixture is a little mealy but there are still chickpea-size chunks of flattened butter remaining. In a separate bowl, whisk together the egg, vinegar and ice cold water. Make a well in the center of the flour, and pour in half the liquid, tossing gently and compressing lightly with your hands until it comes into a shaggy damp ball. Add a little more liquid if the dough is dry, but not too much that the dough is tacky or sticks to your hands. You may not need all the liquid.

Dump the dough out onto a floured surface, divide it in half, shape into disks and wrap the disks in plastic wrap. Place in the fridge to chill for at least 30 minutes while you make the filling.

(continued)

JAMAICAN-STYLE PATTY POT PIES WITH PICKLED SLAW (CONT.)

To make the filling, in a large skillet, heat the olive oil over medium-low heat, add the diced onion, celery, and garlic and cook for 10 to 12 minutes, stirring occasionally, until softened. Add the diced habanero pepper, thyme leaves, curry powder, cumin, allspice and salt, and cook until fragrant, about 2 more minutes. Add the cooked lentils, hot sauce, lemon juice and nutritional yeast to bring it all together. Remove from the stove and allow the mixture to cool completely.

Have 4 lightly oiled 6-inch (15-cm) ramekins nearby. Remove one of the disks from the fridge and, using a floured rolling pin on a floured surface, roll it out into an ⅛-inch (3-mm)-thick round. Using the ramekins as a guide, gently place them on top of the dough and cut 2 inches (5 cm) of extra space around the base of each. Ease the cut dough into the oiled ramekins, making sure to press the crust into the corners. Divide the filling among the ramekins. Pinch the edges of the crusts closed with a fork or your fingers, and place the pies in the freezer for at least 30 minutes, or until you're ready to bake. Repeat with the other half of the dough and rest of the filling.

Preheat the oven to 400°F (200°C or gas mark 6).

Remove the pies from the freezer and bake for 25 to 40 minutes, depending on how frozen they are, until slightly puffed and golden. Serve with the pickled slaw.

NOTE: The hot sauce and lemon juice add a sharp acidity that helps cut through the fat in the pastry. Do not use Tabasco because its flavor is less vinegary and gives more of a harsh heat.

FILLING

3–4 tbsp (45–60 ml) olive oil

1 large yellow onion, diced

6 tbsp (60 g) finely diced celery (about 2 small stalks)

4 cloves garlic, minced

½ habanero or Scotch bonnet pepper, diced

2 sprigs of thyme, stems discarded

1 tsp curry powder

1 tsp ground cumin

½ tsp ground allspice

Salt to taste

2 cups (400 g) cooked green lentils

5–6 dashes of Louisiana hot sauce (or other mild, vinegary hot sauce)

2 tbsp (30 ml) freshly squeezed lemon juice

¼ cup (20 g) nutritional yeast or plain bread crumbs

BAKING BASICS

GENERAL TIPS AND TROUBLESHOOTING

Despite my need for artistic license in the kitchen, when I'm experimentation baking instead of cooking, there are guidelines that have helped me understand the limits of my experimentation. I've adopted these tips through countless mistakes . . . ahem . . . experiences (or extensive Googling). But be advised, sometimes I ignore them, too.

Read each recipe through before beginning so you know you have everything you need and have an idea of how and where each ingredient will be used.

Gather Your Things: Also known as mise en place, a fancy French phrase that means get everything prepped ahead of time and set up on your work station. I'm usually horrible at this, but for people who don't want to get caked flour over their cabinet handles mid-batter mixing because they're trying to find where they put that vial of vanilla, it's a helpful tip—one many pro bakers heavily stress. It also speeds the entire process along.

Testing All Leaveners: Leaveners are essential to getting tall perky buns, muffins, and cakes. Baking soda is a chemical leavener that is extra strong, and baking powder is a mix of baking soda and other things. You should test them to make sure they work by adding a little acid to them and seeing whether they fizz. If they don't fizzle like a third-grade science experiment, toss them out. Yeast is also a wonderful leavener that creates carbon dioxide in bread. Blooming the yeast first gets the whole process started. Add it to warm water with a pinch of sugar, and it should create a frothy foamed cap as it starts to grow. If it doesn't, the yeast is stale, and it should be tossed also.

General Storing: Nuts and certain flours made from nuts or seeds should be kept in the fridge or freezer after opening. Things should generally be kept in an airtight container so they don't go stale or spoil quickly. Things with eggs have a much shorter life span on the counter than, say, crackers, and should be tossed out after a day or two, or frozen. If you live in a relatively cool, dry place—let's say Boston, for instance—some of these deadlines are a little more flexible.

Storing Baked Goods: Be sure to wrap chips and crackers only after they've cooled all the way to room temperature, about 72°F (22°C). Rushing this step can leave you with soggy food later on when the residual steam from cooking gets trapped in the bag or tin with the goodies, moistening them.

Lining and Oiling Pans: This is essential if you eventually want to get the food out of their baking pan successfully. For cakes, I like to oil the pan itself, line it with parchment, and then oil it again. I trace the bottom of my pan on a large enough sheet of parchment paper, and then use scissors to cut inside the line. There are other more fun tricks out there on the Internet, too. Random tip: I love spraying my measure cups with cooking spray before I measure out honey or something else super sticky. It all comes out in one satisfying swoop.

Cooling Wire Racks: Post-bake cooling is especially important for quick breads and cakes. Sometimes slicing them too early can give you a gummy center. Allowing them to cool completely helps the flour absorb any excess moisture in the cake. But for every rule, there's a good time to break them; I like ignoring this step when I want a really gooey cookie straight out of the oven.

Acids and Fats: It took me a while to catch on, but acids such as lemon juice, buttermilk and vinegar should be folded into creams and fats, or they risk curdling and deflating them. Always add flour and buttermilk in batches. This method helps mix all the ingredients well, but it also makes sure the acids have a buffer like flour to stop the butter from curdling again.

Measuring Flour: I fluff the flour in its large container, whether it's the bag it came in or a separate canister. Using the measuring cup, pick up the flour, then drop it back down. Do this a handful of times until the flour granules are light and separated. Then in one big scoop, mound up the measuring cup, being careful not to compress the flour, and then take a knife or your straightened index finger and level off the top.

COOKIE GUIDELINES

The ideal cookie can range from person to person. All of my favorite cookie recipes throughout this book meet certain requirements. I want a cookie that 1) has a chewy inside, 2) has a crusty outside, 3) melts in my mouth and 4) spreads out on the sheet pan without me flattening them myself. To me, that's a wonderful cookie, and if you're also in this family of thinking, approach your cookie batters like so:

The Fat: You can't have a good cookie without fat, whether it's good ol' sweet cream butter or chunky peanut butter. It gives moisture, flavor and tenderness to your cookie. Creaming the butter is the most important step for chewy cookies. The butter should be at room temperature, soft enough to whip without struggle and solid enough to trap the pockets of air in the batter that will later help the cookies rise. Creaming the butter and sugar together as the first step also allows the ingredients that don't mix as well together—that is, sugar and fat (and any binders too)—to get acquainted immediately.

Sugars: A combination of brown sugar and granulated sugar is best. Brown sugar contains molasses, which helps bring moisture to your cookies and makes them spread. Granulated sugar is great for absorbing liquid, creating a crispy edge and nice brown color, and for stopping the strands of gluten in the flour from forming as easily.

Flour: Don't overwork it, or it will be a tough and dry cookie. Don't add too much, or the cookie will crumble or be cakey and struggle to spread.

Any Add-Ins: These get folded in last, right before they go in the oven. I once added crushed oats to a cookie batter and then refrigerated it overnight, only to find out come morning that the oats had absorbed all the liquid in the batter, and I had to piece together hard crumbs on my baking sheet.

Other Cookies: Some cookies need to be crumblier, such as shortbread cookies, or crisper, such as graham crackers. In these instances, a higher ratio of flour to fat and sugar will provide a drier, crumbly cookie. Omitting the brown sugar, which has sticky molasses syrup inside, will give a cookie less chewiness, and replacing the brown sugar with all granulated sugar will make it crisper because granulated sugar absorbs liquid and caramelizes into hard candy under the heat.

Chewy Cookie Trick: I like to rap the tray of my cookies on the countertop a few times right after they come out of the oven; it releases any excess air, creates more cracks and crevices across the surface, and make a denser, chewier cookie overall.

COOKIE TROUBLESHOOTING: WHAT WENT WRONG

Too Dry: If a cookie is too dry or tough, it could mean you either used too much flour in relation to the other ingredients in the recipe or you overworked the gluten in the flour by mixing the batter for too long.

Spreading: If the cookies spread too much, you either used too much fat or too much sugar in the recipe in relation to the amount of flour used. Think of baking caramel sauce: you need enough flour to absorb the liquefied sugar. It could also mean you used too much leavener (baking soda or baking powder) in the recipe.

PIE CRUST AND BISCUIT GUIDELINES

Biscuits are probably my second favorite thing to make, and pies come in at a close third. I always use butter, not a combination of butter and shortening, and the opposite is true of tall, cakey cookies. Most likely, too much flour was added.

I've learned biscuits and pies take about two parts flour and one part cold, solid fat—plus salt and sugar, if using, to enhance the flavors—and then just enough cold liquid to bind the two together without raising the temperature of the fat. Some other things to keep in mind:

Cold Fat: You always want the butter to stay solid/cold and in pieces throughout the flour, because as soon as the heat from the oven finally does melt it, it'll puff up inside the layer of flour encasing it, creating tender and flaked layers. If the butter ever starts to soften during the process, place it in the fridge or freezer for a few minutes to harden. I like to make my biscuits in a metal bowl because it holds cold temperatures well, and I can place the bowl into the freezer at anytime if the butter starts to soften and it'll quickly bring the temperature of the butter back to a workable place.

Less Liquid = Tender Dough: You don't want to add too much water because a higher ratio of liquid to fat makes the dough tough and pliable when baked. Overworking the dough does this, too. So add most of the liquid first, holding back a few tablespoons, gently toss and try to compress into a ball. If the dough is still crumbly, add more water just until the ball feels shaggy but dense.

Wrapping and Refrigerating: There are a couple stages of putting the dough back in the fridge or freezer after handling it. It's all to harden the butter back up.

Even Rolling: If you see cracks in the dough as you roll it, knead the dough a little first to make it more pliable. Apply even pressure as you roll, always pressing from the center and pushing outward. This keeps the crust evenly thick. After every couple of rolls, lift and wiggle the dough to keep it from sticking to the surface. Fold the dough loosely around the rolling pin to help transfer it to a buttered pie dish. Ease it into the dish, crimp the edges together with your fingers and then place the dough in the freezer for 15 minutes to harden again.

The Blender Method: You can make pie crusts in a food processor if you don't like working the butter into the flour with your hands. This keeps the butter from warming as quickly if you also suffer from the hot-hand curse like I do. Just add the flour and salt to the food processor, pulse it to combine, add the chunks of cold fat, pulsing it a few times until the butter is dispersed and the size of chickpeas, then add the water a couple tablespoons (30 ml) at a time, pulsing just until a ball forms on the blade, no longer.

PIE CRUST AND BISCUIT TROUBLESHOOTING: WHAT WENT WRONG

Tough Dough: If you suffer from a biscuit that's hockey-puck-tough or a pie that's almost rubbery, the dough was either overmixed, developing the gluten in the flour, or the fat to flour to water ratio was off.

Shrinking Crust: If your pie crust shrinks, you didn't let the gluten in the dough relax before you baked it. This is also important for yeast breads. For pies, it helps to use pie weights (such as dried beans over foil) or to place the pie in the freezer for 10 to 15 minutes to harden.

MUFFINS AND QUICK BREADS

Muffin Tops: I love it when I can get a muffin that peaks out of a pan and makes a little domed top. To help a muffin achieve that look, place the filled muffin tin into the oven at a higher temperature (about 50°F [30°C] hotter), bake them for 10 or so minutes and then turn the heat down to finish cooking the insides. This extra heat cooks the outside of the muffin first, crusting it over and then as the insides cook, it pushes the dome up and out over the edges.

Quick Breads: I've never taken a bite of a quick bread and just put it down: it's not a thing I do. I love them all. But there are some textures that impress me more than others when I bite into one. I love my breads to be tall and slightly airy, but still tender and full of moisture. The dense breads are delicious, but sometimes too heavy and cakey.

CAKE GUIDELINES

Cakes are a tough category. I have a few things to say, though.

- Make sure the temperature of your ingredients follow the recipe. It sucks when I cream butter and sugar together and then add cold liquid or eggs to the batter. This is a disaster, and a waste of ingredients because it clumps the fat and separates it.

- When it's time to ice, besides the more obvious tip of letting the cake cool completely so the icing stays on the cake and not on the countertop, I like to flip my cakes over and ice them from the bottom. This gives a nice flat surface without needing to cut away and discard any precious bits of cake.

- Don't use a nonstick pan because it can make the sides of the cake bake faster, which can result in a tough outer edge, but if you must, lower the temperature of the oven slightly.

- Don't bake cakes at too high a temperature—use a thermometer. If the temperature is too high, the cake can crack.

- Don't use too much baking soda, or the cake may rise rapidly, then collapse suddenly in the center.

- Cool the cake completely before storing (see the notes above).

- Put cakes in the oven immediately after mixing them, or they can collapse halfway through baking. Cakes with double-acting baking powder and baking soda start rising as soon as the liquid hits them, which means while they're still in batter stage, so keep the wet ingredients separated from the dry ingredients until the very last possible moment.

INGREDIENTS

This is a list of many of the ingredients I use throughout the book, and a breakdown of how I use them and think about them.

FATS

Fats are essential to baking. They give flavor, tenderness, moisture and lift. They even make sure your cakes and pies don't get permanently glued to the pan they're cooked in.

Dairy-Free Butter: Earth Balance Butter Sticks are my go-to dairy-free butter. I love the version that actually comes shaped like sticks, because I don't need to do any messy measuring from the container. I also love that I can easily bring just the right amount of butter to room temperature by just leaving one or two sticks on the countertop overnight. If you want to replace the butter in one of my recipes with something dairy-free, and the recipe asks for the butter to be "softened" or "very cold," it's important to replace it with a fat that behaves the same way at those temperatures. I've found dairy-free butter and coconut oil to be the best substitutes in this case.

Nut Butters: When a recipe is centered around the flavor of a nut butter, such as peanut butter or tahini, I love using it as the primary fat. There's so much delicious oil it provides, and it usually acts as a multipurpose ingredient—naturally binding, flavoring and tenderizing my recipes.

Organic Unrefined Virgin Coconut Oil: This is a natural saturated fat, meaning it stays solid at room temperature, unlike other oils. It is helpful for everything from pies to puffed pastries. I always use unrefined virgin coconut oil. When I'm baking something sweet, I love the creamy tropical flavor it offers. You can make your own coconut oil at home by boiling a can of full-fat coconut milk for an hour or so until the milk cooks off and you're left with nothing but a brownish oil. If the thing I'm making is not sweet, I like to stick to butter, so the coconut flavor isn't out of place. In this case, refined coconut oil would also work—it doesn't taste or smell like coconut—but I personally prefer regular butter to it, because it has more nutrients, depending on the brand.

Extra Virgin Olive Oil: I love the flavor of olive oil, but when dealing with the delicate flavors of flour, it's easy for this oil to become overpowering, and so I only whip it out when I'm celebrating its fruitiness with recipes like my Olive Oil Biscuits (page 58).

Neutral Oils: When I'm adding fat but I don't need it to lift or flavor my baked goods (the effects of butter and olive oil), and instead just add tenderness and moisture, I use a neutral-flavored cooking oil. Grapeseed oil was my most used oil when making these recipes, but sunflower seed oil was my second most used. Safflower oil, canola oil and vegetable oil all work perfectly fine as well.

Cooking Sprays: I always keep cooking spray around to oil my pans quickly and in an even layer. My favorite is coconut oil spray, which is becoming more widely available. I buy Spectrum Naturals or the Trader Joe's brand, but there are lots of different flavors out there. I find the butter-flavored sprays to smell and taste too artificial, and the olive oil sprays to go best with savory recipes, but whichever one you choose will get the job done. You can also make a homemade cooking spray by combining one part fat with three parts water and shaking it up inside a spray bottle, one that gives a nice even mist.

WHEAT FLOURS

These are all the flours (and flour-like powders) I use throughout this book. You'll see me use white whole wheat flour and spelt flour the most, and sometimes I'll use a combination of them or two or three other flours to create a whole new texture. I've found King Arthur brand of flour to offer the most consistent and reliable results when it comes to measuring and weighing them out, and so I'd recommend this brand and even Bob's Red Mill over others, although store-bought brands and Trader Joe's flours work, too. It's all about consistency, and sometimes those little details can affect a recipe a lot.

White Whole Wheat Flour: Many of my recipes call for white whole wheat flour. It's made from white wheat grains, which have a milder flavor and a less grainy texture than regular stone-ground flour made from red wheat. The more traditional flour can sometimes overpower other ingredients. The texture is not as fine as all-purpose white flour, so for some recipes I even mix the two to create the perfect balance. I love using white whole wheat flour with a lot of chocolate recipes because the intensity of the cacao marries well with the tinge of nuttiness the flour gives once it's baked. Chocolate is a powerful flavor that can easily stand up to it.

Whole Wheat Pastry Flour: This is a whole-grain flour that has much less protein than both regular white flour and whole wheat flour. Protein is the gluten, or glue, that's necessary for giving structure and elasticity to certain breads and doughs, so for crusty loaves of bread that require large, spongy pockets of air, it's better to use a heavier glutinous flour. Whole wheat pastry flour has a lower protein percentage than most flours, so it tends to produce a more tender crumb, which is perfect for things like pie crusts, biscuits and fluffy cakes. And these are the exact places I encourage its use.

Spelt Flour: This is also my other go-to, all-purpose whole-grain flour and is even lighter than white whole wheat! It can easily replace white whole wheat in all the recipes it's called for in this book. It's a specialty flour that is harder to find, so I don't always have it around, but when I do buy it and use it, it's amazing. Store it in the fridge or freezer if you buy it in bulk, or keep it in a cool, dry cabinet and use it up soon. I don't think that should be too difficult.

Unbleached All-Purpose Flour: For recipes like chewy yeast breads, I replace at least a fraction of the flour with unbleached all-purpose flour, because using all whole wheat or white whole wheat makes the dough too tough.

GLUTEN-FREE FLOURS

I bake with gluten-free flours a lot because I enjoy the variety of flavors they offer. I've tried to be conscious of people who have gluten intolerances by keeping gluten-free flours separate from wheat flours. All the gluten-free flours I use in the book have a high protein content, making them heavier flours that hold up to the other ingredients, provide good structure and don't need to be combined with other flours or enhancers to perform well. I use these flours only in muffins, cookies, cakes and crackers, though, because trying to create yeast breads that require a durable gluten structure is a whole separate beast of a discussion. The following flours are naturally gluten-free, but check before buying to ensure they're produced in facilities that are careful of cross-contamination.

Gluten-Free All-Purpose Flour: If you are gluten intolerant, you're probably in the habit of adding flour enhancers to gluten-free flour to create structure and elasticity. Gluten-free flour can be used as a stand-in for many of the cake, cookie, cracker and custard pie recipes. Gluten-free flour blends vary drastically across different brands. Some use potato starch or rice flour. I'd find a brand that is consistent that you love and use it here.

Nut Meal Flours (Almond, Hazelnut, Chestnut and Coconut): Nut flours are delicious, and I love using them in muffin recipes because they give the batter an amazing crumb texture, which can sometimes be what makes or breaks a muffin. Nut flours are naturally gluten-free and can even be toasted beforehand to enhance their natural flavors and to toast the oils present. Right now I have so many bags of almond flour (both the meal and the superfine kind), chestnut flour and hazelnut meal flour. You can make a lot of your own nut meals by grinding blanched nuts in a food processor until fine, before it turns to butter.

Rolled Oats and Oat Flour: I love cooking with rolled oats when they're paired with cinnamon. The flavors are a heavenly marriage. I'm not too crazy about oat flour, which to me has a strange taste and smell when it's baked, so I tend not to use it.

Quinoa Flour: This is a great high-protein flour that can also be used interchangeably with chestnut flour or chickpea flour, as these are all heavy flours that can hold up like high-protein gluten flours. Roast this flour for 30 minutes to release its saponin—a natural chemical that gives the flour its strong flavor. Spread the flour on a parchment-lined baking sheet and bake in a 300°F (150°C or gas mark 2) oven for 45 minutes to 1 hour. This will make the flour less sour.

Chickpea Flour/Besan: This is another great high-protein flour that I love to use in place of all-purpose flour when making savory flatbreads or crackers.

Chestnut Flour: I discovered this delicious flour while I lived in Italy. It's mild and nutty, and wonderful in dessert recipes, but it is harder to find in the United States. I have to order it online if I want to taste it again.

Coconut Flour: This is a coarser grain flour, so I only use it for crumbled or press-in pie crusts. It has a wonderful coconut flavor, and so it's great in recipes with ingredients that complement it well.

MISCELLANEOUS

Whole Wheat Phyllo Dough: I love turning to phyllo dough when I want a quick pastry without a lot of work. They are sheets of paper-thin dough made from flour and water. The thinness offers a texture that's even flakier than puffed pastry but without the heaviness of puffed pastry dough because you can control the type and amount of fat you brush between the layers. You can usually find them in the frozen section of a supermarket; just thaw them in the fridge overnight. I actually keep unopened packages in the fridge for weeks, and they never go stale. Once they're opened, though, they're hard to keep from going brittle. Whole wheat phyllo dough can easily be replaced with regular phyllo dough, too.

Nuts: Buy nuts raw and unsalted and toast them before you put them in desserts, or their flavor will fall flat.

Arrowroot Powder (gluten-free): This is a good thickening starch made from a tropical tuber, and it's what I use to replace cornstarch, which just has absolutely no nutritional value. Arrowroot is great for thickening, and needs to be turned into a slurry—just like cornstarch does—before adding it to a liquid recipe.

Tapioca Flour (gluten-free): This is a starch that binds ingredients and, when baked, makes the texture very springy. I use tapioca flour for custards, puddings and fruit pastes.

Agar Agar (gluten-free): Agar agar is a type of dried seaweed that is an amazing replacement for gelatin. It's tasteless and nearly odorless and doesn't need to be refrigerated like gelatin to set. Order it online, find it in health food stores or buy it at Asian markets.

Cocoa Powders (gluten-free): Cacao powder is raw and made from cold-pressed raw cocoa beans. This powder has a very intense flavor. Cocoa powder is roasted cacao powder, so it has less nutrients and a milder flavor. Dutch process cocoa is cocoa powder that's been treated with an alkalizing agent, neutralizing its pH so it's not as reactive to leaveners like baking soda in baked recipes. It's also milder in flavor than the others.

Peanut Butter Powder (gluten-free): I use peanut butter powder in smoothies mostly, but I added it to my Peanut Butter Jelly Bread recipe (page 174). It has much fewer calories and fat than regular peanut butter.

EGGS AND EGG REPLACERS

Eggs: They do so much—they lift everything from sponge cakes to profiteroles; they bind things like cookies, cakes and doughnuts; and they give structure to custards and puddings and richness and density to yeast-risen sweet breads. I'm so fascinated by them, but I also love the challenge of working without eggs. If I do use eggs in a recipe, which is less than 25 percent of the time, assume they are large, cage-free brown eggs. The color and flavor of the yolk is rich and worth the extra expense. Some recipes I share don't need eggs or egg replacers at all, and I never even miss them. (Note: I hate the smell of cooked eggs, so if I can avoid that smell, I do. Therefore, I usually don't brush the tops of my pies with egg wash for this very reason.)

"Flax Egg": This is a really great omega-3 fat slurry I use in many of my chewy recipes like brownies and cookies, and some dense breads that call for yeast. But for quick breads where I appreciate air pockets and a certain amount of sponginess, I'd rather use something much lighter, like pureed fruit. I always make a huge batch of flax egg, because there seems to always be a need for a ladleful in a recipe. I prefer Bob's Red Mill Golden Flax Meal. To me, it has a subtler flavor than brown flax meal, and makes for a vey dense replacement. To make it, combine 1 cup (120 g) of the ground flaxseed (make sure it's ground to release the fibers and linseed oils from the seed—it's what makes it gummy) and add it to a lidded container along with 3 cups (705 ml) of hot water (1:3 ratio) and let it sit on the counter for an hour, stirring occasionally, until it's thick. Or place it in the fridge for up to 1 week. While I use it mostly for binding, if I want the bind plus lift in a recipe, I just add the flax egg and 1 teaspoon of baking powder per 1 cup (120 g) of flour. In recipes, ¼ cup (60 ml) of this flax slurry stands in for 1 egg. Tip: This slurry goes rancid fast, so don't leave it out on the counter too long.

Aquafaba: This magical brine comes from a can of beans; it's the water the beans of legumes were cooked in. Ever since someone discovered it recently, it has changed the lives of people who gave up eggs along with wonderful desserts like sponge cakes and meringues. A 15-ounce (420-g) can has about ¾ cup (177 ml) of aquafaba. Save the chickpeas or legumes and use them in a salad or other dish later on. To use in recipes as an egg replacement, 3 tablespoons (45 ml) of aquafaba equals 1 egg, while 2 tablespoons (30 ml) equals about 1 egg white.

Silken Tofu: I sometimes use silken tofu to replace an egg. It's a lot less dense than a flax egg. Puree a block of silken tofu, after the extra water is discarded, and use ¼ cup (60 g) of the puree per egg in your recipe.

Unsweetened Applesauce: Not only does applesauce help with binding because of the natural pectin in the fruit, but it also doesn't weigh food down like flax eggs might, and, my favorite part, it gives whatever it's added to a really great flavor. I love using it with anything that has cinnamon in the recipe, because it complements this spice so well. You'll see when you try my Oatmeal Cheddar Cheese Moon Pies (page 15); it adds a deep note of flavor that makes the recipe more delicious than if I had added just eggs alone.

Other Fruit Purees: These are added to recipes only when that fruit is mentioned in the title and a star ingredient. For instance, I'm in love with my Mango Lime Coconut Cake (page 163), which uses gorgeous bright and thick mango puree as both a binder in the cake and in the Mango Mousse Icing that gets slathered all around the top and sides.

DAIRY AND DAIRY-FREE

All Milks: Every time I write "milk" in a recipe, I'm 100 percent using a plant-based milk. I stopped cooking with regular milk years ago. Because I never drink the stuff, it's never just hanging around in my fridge. I've fallen in love with the many plant and nut milks out there, and found they give me amazing results. I stick with unsweetened oat milk, flax milk, soymilk or cashew milk because they're creamy and dense. Although I understand how popular and accessible almond milk has become, I've always found it too thin for some baking projects, and I can taste the toasted nut flavor once the recipe is baked, which isn't always desired. For these reasons, flax milk, soy milk and oat milk never noticeably alter the flavor of my batters.

If you have no aversion or allergy to milk, any type of milk you use will be fine in the recipe, just note that a thicker, fuller fat milk will give your recipe more moisture and tenderness.

Buttermilk: This is a great acid that responds well to baking soda in a recipe, helping it activate and subsequently leaven the bread or cake. It makes an amazing addition to a scone, biscuit, muffin and cake recipes, simply because it creates a tender crumb and a nice rise. But it also offers a tang that complements a pastry's sweetness really well, and so I love adding it.

Un-buttermilk: When I want to make something dairy-free, it's really simple to make a buttermilk stand-in. Again, this works best with a thicker plant-based milk like oat or flax. Just add about 1 tablespoon (15 ml) of acid, like lemon juice, lime juice or vinegar, per 1 cup (235 ml) of the milk called for in the recipe, and allow the milk to sit and curdle for about 5 minutes. Then proceed with the recipe. You can use this trick with regular milk, too.

Full-Fat Canned Coconut Milk: This is a wonderful ingredient that adds thickness, richness, body and flavor to sauces and creams. When I'm replacing heavy cream, this is my go-to. I whip it with sugar to create coconut whipped cream that can top my cakes or pies, and I use it to finish off caramel sauces. I keep the cans in the fridge, because I always seem to need cold coconut milk more often than not for whipping, and it's easy and quick to warm it up if I need it liquefied in a recipe. Without shaking the can, remove it from the fridge, tip it upside down and open the can from the bottom—usually the cream solidifies at the top—and then pour out the water that hasn't solidified (this part doesn't whip, but save it for other recipes or to drink). Once the liquid is gone, you can easily scoop out the cream. I add this directly to a bowl with confectioners' sugar or cane sugar, give it a whip with a hand mixer, and BAM! it's thick and beautiful.

Sometimes I've struggled with getting the whipped cream to come together, and this is because some brands aren't as consistent with their product. If your coconut cream isn't coming together, add a bit of tapioca flour or potato flour during whipping.

Yogurt and Sour Cream: I love using yogurt in recipes, especially muffins and quick breads, because I always have it around. We rarely keep sour cream around, because Eric has a strong disdain for it. I'll never understand, but still, I love working with the things I have available to me. Yogurt does many of the things buttermilk does: it provides a great tangy flavor, acidity and lots of moisture, giving me a tender crumb that's far from dry.

SUGARS

Pure Cane Sugar: I used to live under the delusion that pure cane sugar was better for you than regular (granulated) sugar. It's true that the more unprocessed the sugar is and the darker its color, the more likely it is to have more nutrients, but the bottom line is, it's still sugar. The other bottom line is, we can allow ourselves to have it every once in a while.

Brown Sugar: This is just a mix of granulated sugar and molasses. You can make your own by combining 1 cup (200 g) of granulated sugar with 1 tablespoon (20 g) of molasses. I also like to use coconut sugar or muscovado sugar in place of brown sugar.

Coconut Sugar: This has a delicious toasty flavor that makes a good replacement for brown sugar in a recipe. It has a finer grain, which I really love, and if I'm using it in a cookie recipe to replace the brown sugar, I add a bit of molasses to help the cookie spread.

Raw Sugar: I love to use this sugar as a finishing sugar. It gives a great crunch to the tops of biscuits and certain cookies.

LIQUID SWEETENERS

Maple Syrup: Grade B maple syrup is a more concentrated form of Grade A that has been boiled down to help thicken it. It has a darker color and a deeper flavor, but is equal in sweetness to Grade A.

Honey: I use honey when the flavor complements the other ingredients in the recipe. You can also get different kinds. Honey is not vegan, but it can be replaced 1:1 with agave, although the flavor won't taste as floral.

Light and Dark Agave: I use these when I want a mild-flavored liquid sweetener. It's also lower in calories than both honey and maple syrup.

Molasses: Ever since I bought my first jar of molasses a couple of years ago, I have put it in everything. It has a deep malty flavor that goes well with chocolate and ginger plus some orange- or citrus-flavored recipes. I use it in my Coconut Lemongrass Tart with Gingerbread Graham Cracker Crust (page 166) and in some chocolate chip cookies.

EQUIPMENT

Bread Knife: My favorite piece of equipment is a serrated bread knife. This is a tool I cannot live without. In fact, I have lived a very miserable life without it, and will never choose that life again. I have a Mercer 10-inch (25.4-cm) bread knife that's made from high-carbon Japanese steel and it cuts through my quick breads (and regular breads) like butter. I am in love.

Box Grater: This is really great for shredding softer things like zucchini for my Zucchini Bread (page 146) or even shredding cold (but not frozen) butter on mornings I forgot to leave it on the counter to soften overnight.

Wire Racks: These are for cooling things quickly because they're propped up on little legs and full of holes that allow air to get in and underneath the baked good.

Cast-Iron Skillet: I have never let go of my 8-inch (20-cm) cast-iron pan and I make so many things in it. It's not the standard 12-inch (30-cm) size, but it works for me, and it always gives my breads a beautiful crust.

Measuring Spoons and Cups: Because you can't do any baking without these.

Cookie Cutters and Biscuit Cutters: I use my 2-inch (5-cm) cookie/biscuit cutter the most.

Bench Scraper: This is used for cutting dough, but mostly for scraping the surface of the counter of solidified bits of wet, slurried flour—it can cling to things for dear life. On second thought, maybe you should get a second one to scrape kitchen tiles, too; they're gentle enough.

Rolling Pins: For years I just used the fat end of an empty wine bottle wrapped in plastic wrap, but if you fancy, get the standard kind. Eventually, I want to get a handle-less rolling pin that tapers at the edges. It'd be great for not pinching the dough.

Thermometers: I work with a hot oven. It's actually gotten me into a lot of trouble when telling people how to re-create foods in their own homes using the steps I used. It just helps us stay on the same page.

Whisks: I have a handheld whisk for casually declumping masses of food on the stove top, and I have an electric handheld whisk for small-batch quick-whipping. Then I have the whisk attachment that came with my stand mixer. They're all great.

Standard 12-Cup Muffin Tin: I make many things in this, from buns to muffins to mini cakes. It's also a great tool to give a nice lift and crust to cake recipes. The heat from the sides of the pan help the batter rise because it comes into contact with more of the surface area of the cooking item.

Scale: I wanted to fight this purchase, but ultimately it's been fun weighing everything from fruit to spices.

OTHER EQUIPMENT YOU WILL NEED

- Quarter sheet pan or half rimmed baking sheet
- One 9-inch (23-cm) springform cake pan
- Two standard 9-inch (23-cm) cake pans
- Two 9 x 5-inch (23 x 12.5-cm) loaf pans
- One 4 x 14-inch (10 x 35.6-cm) tart pan
- Two 9-inch (23-cm) round tart pans
- Stand mixer and electric hand mixer
- Blender and food processor
- Saucepans in small, medium and large sizes
- One small and one large deep-dish skillet

ACKNOWLEDGMENTS

Thank you to my partner in crime and favorite human, Eric Harrison, for always being by my side. You were and always are my main source of support and encouragement every day, and you were a mirror for me while I worked through this difficult but transformative project. Thank you to Page Street Publishing and the entire team—especially William, Marissa and Meg—for helping me refine my first cookbook vision. Thank you to my incredible family—every single person: my cousins, aunts, uncles and, of course, my mom and dad for retelling their childhood stories over the phone to me to give me even more inspiration *and* giving me permission to tell our collective stories. Thank you to my wonderful friends on Instagram for their continued support, positive energy and daily food inspiration, and my friend, Lynessa Brown-Brown, for reminding me of my reason for writing this book in the first place. Thank you to my friends and mentors, Rusty Hill, Lisa Bolin and Paige Fletcher, for showing me the ropes. And again, thank you to my ma for shipping me all of those baking care packages across the country to remind me you were always available to help in any way as I got lost in my kitchen for more than three months. And finally, thank you to all the people who touched my life in ways you may not have even realized and inspired the stories and thoughts throughout.

ABOUT THE AUTHOR

Jerrelle Guy is an award-winning food photographer, recipe contributor and Tastemade Tastemaker. She's a recent graduate of Boston University with a master's in gastronomy, and received her BFA in illustration from the Rhode Island School of Design. She now lives in Boston with her loving partner and cross-eyed cat, Christopher.

INDEX